1979, 1980
Owner of "Jet Dance"
out of Jet Deck Daughter
our 2nd race horse — SI 106
Stakes winner of 120,000 in Colo & California

**Easy Jet**
*(1967-1992)*

Raw speed and courage,
tempered by a sure hand.

He ran the good race,
As only a champion can.

A LOFT ENTERPRISES BOOK

# WIRE TO WIRE

## THE WALTER MERRICK STORY

By Frank Holmes

The authorized biography of the Dean of the Quarter Racehorse Men

# WIRE TO WIRE

*Published by*

## LOFT
**ENTERPRISES**

13352 Meridian Road
Elbert, CO 80106

*Design, Typography, and Production*
**Sandy Cochran Graphic Design**
Fort Collins, Colorado

*Prologue Ink Drawings*
**Mike Craig**

*Back Cover Painting*
**Orren Mixer**

*Printing*
**Vision Graphics**
Loveland, Colorado

*First Printing: October 2001*

ISBN 0-9714998-0-2

# DEDICATION

This book is dedicated to Onna Christien Shinn Merrick

"Tien"

As wife, mother, partner and friend,
she's been with me every step of the way.

*Walter Merrick*

# I N T R O D U C T I O N

## By Gary Vorhes

I guess the best way to explain my reverence for Walter Merrick is to say that I rank the day I spent with him right alongside the morning I spent with Louis L'Amour. Both men are legends.

Our magazine story about Walter and the 14 Ranch was published in May of 1990. To gather the information and the photographs, I drove to Sayre, Oklahoma. Walter, his wife, son, and son-in-law were unfailingly gracious and patient, and I was pretty overwhelmed with the size of the operation, for openers.

Although some journalists try to appear hardened and cynical in the presence of famous people, I certainly didn't feel that way. And when Walter led Easy Jet out on the lawn for me to photograph, I was flat overloaded. Even at an advanced age, the horse hardly seemed to touch the ground.

And the pictures I took didn't really capture the striking look I saw in the eyes of the horse, and in the eyes of the man. It's been described as "the look of eagles."

Walter and Easy Jet's accomplishments at the race track are chronicled here, but you may be surprised to learn that Merrick began his life "out with the wagon," cowboying. He never let go of that heritage, but he always had an eye for a horse with some speed.

As I quoted him back in 1990, "In those days (the Depression years), there wasn't much market for a horse that couldn't do anything except run. I always liked a good, fast horse — one that could run when you needed him to."

Today, Walter's eye and the blood of Easy Jet and other speedsters from the Merrick operation have given us lots of horses who can run, and want to.

I might add another little sidelight to you who are about to learn the Walter Merrick story. As he worked on this book, I watched Frank Holmes become more and more enthused and filled with admiration for the man and what he had accomplished. Frank's appreciation grew stronger with each visit and each new chapter.

So, now you, too, can have a chance to join those who know and admire Walter Merrick, a man who just makes you proud to wear a western hat.

Walter Merrick defines the word "horseman."

Gary Vorhes
Editor in Chief
Western Horseman

# Gauging Speed

## The Evolution of Quarter Horse Race Ratings

Because Wire to Wire is first and foremost the story of Walter Merrick and his Quarter racehorses, an up-front look at the differing ways that sprinting performances have been rated during the last half-century is in order.

The dawn of organized Quarter Horse racing came in the mid-1940s with the formation of the Arizona-based American Quarter Racing Association (AQRA). Not a blood registry, its main purpose was to identify horses for racing purposes and establish a method by which their performances could be measured.

The system AQRA came up with designated certain times within each of seven recognized distances-220 to 440 yards-as either D, C, B, A or AA.

At the beginning, horses that achieved A or AA ratings were designated Register of Merit (ROM) racehorses. By 1950, the times had improved to the point that a AAA rating was added, and only horses who ran AA time or better earned ROMs. Soon, even that wasn't enough, and AAA+ and AAAT (for "top") ratings were added.

In 1969, the lettered grade rating system was dropped in favor of a more-exacting numerical speed index system. In this system, which is still in effect, to qualify for what had been the old AA rating, a Quarter runner must achieve a speed index of 80. To qualify for the old AAA rating, he must achieve a speed index of 90.

To date, the highest speed index ever recorded at the classic Quarter Horse distance of 440 yards was the 128 registered by Evening Snow at Turf Paradise in Phoenix, Arizona, in 1996.

Coincidentally, the change from the old lettered system to the new numerical system occurred during Easy Jet's freshman year on the track. He began the year with a AAAT rating and ended it with a speed index of 100.

To dyed-in-the-wool Quarter racehorse men like Walter Merrick, however, speed ratings have never been the ultimate goal. Crossing the finish line first has.

# ACKNOWLEDGMENTS

The writing of *Wire to Wire* was a long time in the making. Walter first approached me about the project four years ago. For one reason or another, it was pushed back until the spring of 2001. Even with that long of an incubation period there were numerous obstacles to overcome. The first dealt with the man himself.

Anyone who's ever been around Walter knows that he is not the most talkative human who ever lived. At one point early in the interviewing process, I felt obligated to remind him that I could not write his biography using one-word answers. As the process wore on and he became more at ease, he obliged me with more complete reflective and insightful responses. The net result is a rare "up close and personal" look at the remarkable life of a remarkable man.

Then, too, anyone who has ever spent any time around Walter knows that he is extremely soft-spoken. When I went to have my first interview tapes transcribed, Walter's voice was all but inaudible. So I did what any desperate author would do to move the project forward. I wired him for sound. One way or another, we got it done.

As is always the case in a project like this, I was fortunate to receive the help of numerous people. I take this opportunity to thank them for their assistance. Don Treadway and his customer-service crew at AQHA (American Quarter Horse Association) in Amarillo, Texas—most notably Tammy Garrison—cheerfully and quickly provided reams of production records on all of the great sires and dams that Walter has been associated with. It was a major task—Easy Jet's computer records alone were larger than most cities' Yellow Pages—and it was much appreciated.

Jim Jennings' editorial folks at *The Quarter Horse Journal* and *Quarter Racing Journal* were also extremely cooperative. Tawanna Walker was always the picture of good-natured professionalism in her efforts to help me locate scores of the photographs that appear in this book. To her credit, she never once threatened my life.

David Hoover at the American Quarter Horse Heritage Center & Museum was also of tremendous help. David set me up to research a number of early AQHA registration files and thereby come up with even more priceless photographs. J. W. Rossen and Ed Davis of Erick, Oklahoma, Richard Louden and Billie Fox of Trinidad, Colorado, and Judy Tracy and J. W. Chalfant of Cheyenne, Oklahoma, dug through their personal archives to come up with photos that appear in Part I.

Photographs are an integral part of any book that attempts to capture the visual flavor of a bygone era. I hope you will agree with me that the 200-plus photos that appear in Wire to Wire are an amazing collection that serves to document forever one of the most colorful chapters in the history of the American West.

Finally, heartfelt thanks and deep appreciation to the entire LOFT crew. Without them, this whole project would still be on the drawing board and I'd still be trying to locate a pencil.

*Frank Holmes*

# TABLE OF CONTENTS

# PART 1

# A CHILD
# OF
# THE TIMES

# THE CHRISTMAS CLOCK

Wheeler County, Texas

Christmas Eve, 1918

The boy stood at the foot of his bed. He wasn't sure he believed in Santa Claus, or in presents that miraculously appeared overnight.

It was hard to believe in anything.

His father lay bed-ridden in town, stricken by the deadly flu epidemic that had paralyzed the entire country. His oldest sister had died of typhoid fever the fall before and his oldest brother had been badly wounded in the war.

And yet, he wanted to believe in something.

So he took a sock from the only good pair he owned, tacked it to the foot of the bed and crawled under the covers. Doubt crept into his mind once more, so he got up and put his alarm clock in the sock—just to make sure there would be something in it when he woke up.

In the middle of the night, the boy's mother came to his room. She gently woke him and told him to get dressed, go to the barn and hitch up the wagon team. His father had suffered a relapse, and wasn't expected to live through the night.

He jumped out of bed, slipped on one sock and reached for the other. He retrieved it, only to discover that the clock was stuck inside. He struggled and struggled to get it out. Finally he succeeded, but not before he had ruined the sock. He threw it and the rest of his clothes on and headed for the barn.

Christmas Eve, 1918

It wasn't the best of times for a boy of 7 to grow up in. But grow up he did—at a rate faster than a boy should have to.

Molded by hard times spent in a harsh land, the boy grew into the kind of man who would meet the challenges life threw at him with outward calm and inner resolve. The kind of man who would keep his feet planted firmly on the ground while reaching for the stars. The kind of man who would become first a leader and then a legend.

He grew up to be Walter Merrick.

Original Artwork by Mike Craig

# THE DIE IS CAST

*"I guess that's when I figured out I was going to be a cowboy,*
*and I was going to own and ride some good horses."*
—Walter Merrick

**"She was the first horse I ever owned, and I named her Eight Dollars."**

IF EVER a man was shaped and molded by the times into which he was born, that man is Walter Merrick.

The youngest of five children born to John and Fannie Lou Merrick, Walter Franklin Merrick came into the world on October 5, 1911, in Wheeler County, Texas. He was born at home, on the family's 320-acre farm located 20 miles north of the town of Shamrock.

At the time of Walter's birth, Wheeler County was only one short generation removed from the days of the open range. Nearby Oklahoma was just as unsettled, having been admitted to the Union a mere six years earlier. Prior to that, it had been known simply as "Indian Territory."

Life "down on the farm" in both states was stark and primitive. Electricity and indoor plumbing were a rarity in the rural homes of the area, meaning there was no central heat and air conditioning; no telephones, televisions, radios, refrigerators, washers or dryers. Kerosene lamps, wood- and coal-burning stoves, wash tubs and scrub boards were the order of the day. Automobiles were unheard of in the region's outlying areas. Horses and horse-drawn buggies and wagons were still the primary means of getting around.

There was no Social Security or Medicare — no social assistance of any kind to speak of. Gainful employment, if available, paid anywhere from $1.50 a day for an experienced carpenter, to $1.00 a day for a ranch or farm hand. A cotton picker earned 25 cents per hundred-weight.

But for all they lacked in material comforts and career opportunities, the pioneer farmers and ranchers who occupied the eastern portion of the Texas panhandle and the western edge of Oklahoma made up for it with their boundless energy and hardiness. Within their souls they kindled the pioneer spirit that decreed, "No matter how little I have, I'll make do. Whatever it takes to survive, I'll find the way."

Walter was not merely the youngest member of the Merrick clan; he was the youngest by far. Henry, Clyde, Callie and Ruby — his two brothers and two sisters — were from seven to 20 years older. This disparity played a major role in Walter's upbringing, impacting both where and how he was raised.

"I was only a couple of years old when my brothers left home to go to work for the Davis Brothers' Figure 2 Ranch," Merrick says. "It was a huge, 65-section ranch that sort of surrounded our little place.

"In September of 1916, we lost Callie to typhoid fever. Shortly thereafter, we moved into the nearby town of Texola, Oklahoma, so Ruby could attend school there. My father continued to live at the farm, and we'd spend weekends, holidays and summers there. But during the school year we lived in town."

It was during this time — about when he reached school age — that Walter Merrick's path turned away from following in his father's footsteps as a farmer. It turned instead down a trail dotted with cattle and horses — a trail, according to him, that he was destined to travel.

"My father wasn't a cowboy," Walter says, "he was a farmer. But he farmed with horses and he took a lot of pride in his teams. He generally kept around six head, mostly of Percheron breeding, and he kept them in good shape. But he was never interested in riding horses or racehorses, so we never had any.

"When I was maybe 3 or 4 years old," he says, "I can remember walking out to the fence and watching the Davis Ranch cowboys ride by, driving huge herds of cattle.

"Sometimes, those boys would ride over to the fence and visit with me. I got a chance to get acquainted with them and their horses, and I guess that's when I first figured out what I was going to be when I grew up. I was going to be a cowboy, and I was going to own and ride some good horses."

After relocating to Texola, young Merrick found another likely spot to further his new-found interest in horses.

"Back in the early 1900s," he says, "there weren't a lot of automobiles in our part of the country. When people came to town to sell their crops or pick up supplies, it was either on horseback or in a horse-drawn buggy or wagon. Some of them came from such a distance that they had to stay overnight. When they did, they

*This 1902 photo of Erick, Oklahoma's main street offers a revealing look at the type of small community that young Walter Merrick called home.*

**Photo courtesy 100th Meridian Museum, Sayre, Oklahoma**

needed a place to put their horses up, and park their buggies and wagons.

"Every town had a 'wagon yard' for that purpose, and Texola was no exception. I'd hang around the wagon yard there. It was run by an elderly gentleman that everyone called 'Wooly.'

"I'd go down to the yard just about every day. I'd hang around there and talk to the folks about their horses. And I'd give Wooly a hand when he was taking care of them. He could have run me off, I guess, but he didn't. He just let me hang around, and I was able to pick up a lot of pointers about handling horses as a result."

Shortly after moving to Texola, Walter Merrick also found a way to do more than just hang around horses; he found a way to own one.

"One of my best friends in town was a man named Elmer Renner," he says. "He was a prize fighter and a deputy sheriff, and he farmed a little on the side. He kept his horses and mules in town, in a little set of sheds and corrals.

"I was in about the second grade at the time, and I used to hang around Mr. Renner's corrals. In addition to his work horses, he had some nice saddle geldings that he'd let me ride around town. One of them was a gelding named 'Olin,' and I used to ride him a lot.

"Mr. Renner always encouraged me to match him in races against the other kids' horses. I did that until I'd beaten about every kid and horse in town. Olin was my first match racehorse, but I never ran him for money or anything like that. Just for the fun of it.

"Mr. Renner also had a nice little 2-year-old bay filly that I took a liking to. One day I asked him how much he'd take for her. 'I don't know, Walter,' he said, 'how much have you got?'

"I'd been doing some odd-jobs around town — washing dishes at the local hotel mostly — and had managed to sock away eight dollars. When I told him that, he said, 'Well, I'll just take that for her.'

"She was the first horse I ever

*Walter received his first tangible exposure to horses at a wagon yard similar to the KY Wagon Yard of Sayre, Oklahoma. Proprietor Ben Caudill is the second person from the left in this 1911 photo. He is surrounded by his wife and eight children.*

**Photo courtesy Bob Caudill**

*In addition to the wagon yard, the Caudill family also owned and operated a livery stable and restaurant. It was at an eating establishment like the one pictured here that 10-year-old Walter earned the cash to purchase his first horse.*

**Photo courtesy Bob Caudill**

owned, and I named her Eight Dollars. I broke her to ride bareback, because I didn't own a saddle. I rode her all around town for a couple of years, like a kid would do. When we moved to Colorado, I sold her for $50."

For the three years that he lived in Texola, Walter Merrick managed to enjoy a relatively normal life for that day and age . His life was family farm and small town-based and somewhat isolated as a result. It was a life that revolved, for the most part, around eking out an existence. Travel was, out of necessity, restricted. When it was undertaken, it was usually to conduct some form of business.

Milk and beef cows, hogs, chickens and the family garden plot produced the lion's share of the Merrick family's food. Those products that could not be home-raised or made, such as flour, sugar, coffee, hardware and some clothing, were obtained through the

selling of the two main crops of the day — cotton and broomcorn. Hogs and wheat provided some supplemental income.

As was considered normal for that time, the Merrick family probably did not handle more than $500 a year in cold, hard cash. Money was just not very plentiful.

But family unity was, a solid work ethic was, and early maturity and acceptance of responsibility was. Walter Merrick had been raised to abide by all three tenets, and, as it soon turned out, it was a good thing that he had. By the time he reached age 11, a family tragedy occurred that made it necessary for him to put them into everyday use.

Several years before the Merricks moved to Texola, Walter's two brothers, Henry and Clyde, had quit the Davis Ranch and moved to Trinchera, Colorado. There, Henry filed a homestead claim on a section of

*John Merrick, Walter's father, was stricken by the flu during the pandemic of 1918. He survived, but the aftereffects of the debilitating disease are apparent in this mid-1920s photo.*

land and began making the necessary improvements — known as "proving" the claim up — to ensure the land became permanently his. Both he and Clyde also went to work for John Ballard's Box Ranch, one of the area's larger cattle operations. In 1914, World War I broke out in Europe. Three years later, when it became impossible to remain uninvolved, the United States entered the fray. Henry was inducted into the Army and shipped overseas. Clyde followed in a matter of months.

Although it entered the conflict late, America experienced heavy losses. Of the one million men it sent overseas, more than 100,000 failed to return. On November 11, 1918, the armistice was signed, and Henry, who had been seriously wounded by shrapnel, returned to Colorado. Clyde came home to Oklahoma.

Peace may have come to Western Europe, but not to western Oklahoma. It, like much of the rest of America, was locked in mortal combat with one of the most deadly flu epidemics of all time.

Worldwide, the Spanish Influenza pandemic of 1918 killed at least 21 million people — well over twice the number of combat deaths in all the war. It first appeared in the United States in the spring of 1918. By November, 600,000 Americans had died.

The virus was exceptionally virulent, turning people black and blue and killing them in a matter of hours. In October alone, 195,000 died in this country. Society began to break down. People were afraid to leave their homes for fear of contracting the disease. Industry

*Fannie Lou Merrick, Walter's mother, outlived her husband by more than two decades. She is shown here in 1936 with 3-year-old Jimmie Merrick, Walter's oldest child.*

came to a standstill and homeless children roamed the cities.

In Texola, people were dying so fast there weren't enough caskets available to bury them. Even if there had been, there weren't enough able-bodied men to dig the graves.

John Merrick, Walter's father, was one of the afflicted. Although he survived, he never regained his full health. From that point on, he was never able to work and provide for his family. In order to survive, the Merricks had to turn to each other for help. And 7-year-old Walter was expected to shoulder his share of the load.

"After Henry and Clyde returned from the war," he says, "my parents decided we should all join Henry in Colorado. They thought the higher altitude would be easier on my father.

"By this time, Ruby had married a cowboy named Curtis Willoughby. She and the folks made the trip to Trinchera first, and Curtis and I followed four or five days later.

"We traveled by train, north through the Texas panhandle, then west across the 'high-low' country of northern New Mexico, to Des Moines. From there we turned north again through Folsom, New Mexico, and Branson, Colorado, then west again to Trinchera. We weren't too far south of Trinchera when I looked over the plains and saw herd after herd of horses.

"I asked Curtis who they belonged to, and he said, 'Nobody. They're wild horses.' I lit up like a Christmas tree, and said to myself, 'I'm just going to catch me some of those horses.' And before long, I did."

# 2 WILD HORSES AND ROUGH STRINGS

*"When I got to Trinchera, my childhood was over;
from that point on I had to be a man."*
—Walter Merrick

FOR 9-YEAR-OLD Walter Merrick, life in Trinchera, Colorado, was totally different than life in Texola, Oklahoma. In Oklahoma, before his father's debilitating illness, he had been allowed to be a child. In Colorado, with his father essentially an invalid, he was expected to become both a man and a breadwinner.

"Trinchera was a small, mostly-Mexican community of around 1,000

*In 1918, the Merrick family, including 9-year-old Walter, moved from Texola, Oklahoma, to Trinchera, Colorado. Upon their arrival, they took up residence in this relatively spacious home.*

people," Walter says. "It was situated in ranch country, around 50 miles east of Trinidad. It was a less prosperous town than Texola and harder to make a living in.

"Not that it mattered that much. My dad couldn't work anyway. After he got sick, he had a lot of trouble with his lungs. He just couldn't exert himself very much. So, it was up to me to do what I could."

Even by the standards of the day, which put a premium on hard work and learning to shoulder responsibility at an early age, the burden placed on young Walter was a heavy one. Upon leaving Oklahoma, his parents had sold the farm and livestock. This provided them with the cash to make the move and set up residence in a small rented house in Trinchera.

Making a day-to-day living, however, was another matter.

"After Henry returned from the war," Walter says, "he went back to work for the Box Ranch and even wound up marrying Clara Ballard, the boss's daughter. Henry had been badly wounded by shrapnel, though, and was kind of bent over. He couldn't straighten up. It got to the point where

*The lariat tells the story in this rare photo of a teenaged Walter Merrick stepping up on a young Colorado mustang. The wiry wild horse had obviously been gentled enough that he could be caught, tacked up and mounted without the use of the snubbing post.*

ranch work was too strenuous for him, so he and Clara moved to town and started up a general store.

"The store carried everything from groceries to sewing material, from hardware to leather and harness goods. To help support my family, I worked for Henry before and after school, and on the weekends. He hardly ever paid me with cash, though. Most of the time I drew my wages in the form of groceries or any other staples that we needed.

"Henry had a milk cow and some chickens, and I helped take care of them, too, for a share of the milk and eggs. I guess I worked pretty hard as a kid, but I never really questioned it. It was how I'd been raised. I just did whatever it took to get by."

Even with all his newfound responsibilities, Walter still found time to keep a promise he had made to

himself—and have a little fun in the process.

He became the leader of the "wild horse gang."

"After I started school in Trinchera," he says, "I made friends with Edward Hollenbeck and Buck Couch, a couple of boys my age.

"Edward's family had a small ranch on the north edge of town. They raised some cattle and horses there, and a lot of alfalfa hay. Buck didn't have much family. He lived across the street from us with his mother. She was kind of a sickly lady and died shortly after we arrived in Colorado. Buck moved in with us then, and my folks kind of raised him.

"Not long after we settled in Trinchera, I managed to buy myself a riding horse and a saddle. Edward and Buck had mounts of their own. I told those boys about all those wild horses

*C. P. "Clarence" Newcomb (left), owner of the Butcher Block Ranch of Trinchera, gave 14-year-old Walter Merrick his first full-time job as a cowboy. In this 1928 photo, the prominent Southern Colorado stockman is shown with fellow ranchers Ben Lang and Dick Louden.*

**Photo courtesy Richard Louden**

*Here's the full Butcher Block chuckwagon roundup crew. Seventeen-year-old Walter Merrick is the second cowboy from the left— the one bent over his grub. Walter's good friend Dave Newcomb is the fourth man from the left and C. P. Newcomb is to the far right—under the tent, sitting on a bunkroll.*

**Photo courtesy Richard Louden**

I'd seen from the train, and how I aimed to capture some of them. They thought it sounded like fun and threw in with me."

Once the decision to become wild horse hunters was made, the three friends quickly formulated and put into effect a recurring plan of attack. They would surround a herd of 30 or more horses and haze them into either the Hollenbeck Ranch corrals or the Trinchera shipping yard corrals. Once the herd was captured, the boys— particularly Walter and Buck—would saddle the more likely prospects and take turns trying to ride them.

"There wasn't much to do in Trinchera," Walter says. "About the only recreation we had was chasing those wild horses. We'd corral a bunch of them and buck them out—just play with them.

"Later on, when we got a little better at it, we might take a particularly nice young stallion, geld him and completely break him. We got to where we could turn out a fairly well-broke horse, and when we did we could usually sell it for $50 or so.

"But most of the horses we just played with for a couple of days and then turned them back out.

"When we first started trying to ride those horses, I hit the ground pretty regular," Walter says. "But after three years of practicing, it got to where I had learned how to stay aboard. In fact, it got to where I didn't think I could be thrown.

"Playing with those broncs might have started out as recreation, but it turned into on-the-job training for me. It was where I really learned to ride rough stock, and that opened the door to the first real job that I ever had."

By the time 1926 rolled around, it became apparent to then 15-year-old Walter that working part-time for his brother was not going to provide for all of his family's needs. He was going to have to find a full-time job. When an opportunity to do that presented itself, he was quick to take advantage of it.

"I was working in Henry's store one day in 1926," Walter says. "It must have been during the early part of May, because the ranchers were all coming in to buy their chuck wagon supplies.

"Mr. C. P. Newcomb owned the Butcher Block, one of the largest ranches in that part of the country. I sort of knew him and he knew me. He came into the store that day to buy his supplies and I walked up to him and said, 'Mr. Newcomb, I'm needing a full-time job. Do you have any work for me?'

" 'I don't know, Walter,' he said. 'I can use another cowboy, but I'm not sure you can ride our horses.'

"He looked over at Henry, who was standing nearby, sort of to ask his opinion. Henry just nodded his head up and down. He'd seen me on

**The job that C. P. "Clarence" Newcomb offered Walter was that of a full-time cowboy.**

enough of those wild horses to know I could ride about anything.

"So, Mr. Newcomb said, 'Okay Walter, I'll give you a try. Go and get your saddle and bedroll, and you can ride back out to the ranch with me.' "

The job that C. P. "Clarence" Newcomb offered Walter was that of a full-time cowboy. It paid $45 a month, and for those wages Walter was expected to join up with the ranch's wagon crew and stay with it for the remainder of the spring, summer and fall.

The wagon crew—so called because of the fully-supplied chuck wagon that always accompanied it—was generally comprised of 15 cowboys and 150 saddle horses. Their job, 24 hours a day, seven days a week, was to work the thousands of Butcher Block cattle that ran free over the country's open range.

In the spring and summer months, the cowboys would bunch up, brand, castrate and doctor the herd. In the fall, they would gather animals to be shipped to market. It was the type of life that young Merrick had been itching to take a crack at for years. Before he could settle in to it, however, one last obstacle presented itself.

*The Butcher Block remuda, gathered inside a rope corral, awaits the day's work. The ranch brand, ♀ , appeared on horses and cattle alike.*

**Photo courtesy Billie Fox**

*Life on the open range was often wild and wooly. Even though he's lost his stirrup in this candid photo, the unidentified rough string rider has enough confidence to "fan" his spirited mount. That's Dave Newcomb on the Paint to the far right, looking as if he's enjoying the show.*

**Photo courtesy Billie Fox**

"I was in the eighth grade when I hit Mr. Newcomb up for a job," Walter says. "School hadn't let out for the summer yet, but I went on out to the ranch with him anyway. He took me out to the crew that I was going to be working on and left me there. At noon on that first day, we had broke for lunch when we spotted a trail of dust coming from the direction of town.

"As it got closer, we could see that it was a Model T car. The car pulled up a little short of the camp and a man got out. It was Harold Cox, my school principal. I got kind of embarrassed. I was the youngest hand on the crew, and here my principal was coming all the way from town to see me on my first day of work. There was nothing I could do but go see what he wanted.

"I walked up to the car and he told me, 'Walter, you've got to come back and finish this school term or I can't give you your eighth-grade diploma.'

"There was only about two weeks left of school, but I said, 'Mr. Cox, if I come back, I don't know if this job will be waiting for me when school's out. And I need this job. I need to help

support my mother and father.' So I didn't go back, and I didn't get my diploma."

With his formal education officially over, Walter settled quickly into the routine of being a cowboy. It was a routine that meant getting up at the crack of dawn, a quick breakfast of bacon, gravy, biscuits and coffee, followed by the gathering and saddling up of the day's mounts.

"We always turned the saddle horses out at night," Walter says. "A cowboy, known as a 'nighthawk,' would usually stay with them throughout the night to keep the wild horses from luring them off.

"Come morning, we'd drive them into a big, square rope corral. All it was, really, was some rope stretched tight on all four sides, around 30 inches off the ground. Once we had the horses gathered up inside, one cowboy would walk around the outside of the corral and rope whichever horses were due to be rode that day.

"Catching those horses was kind of an art. You had to do it with a minimum of motion so you wouldn't rile the herd. You had to throw what was known as a hoolihan loop. You'd hold the loop out in front of you, in a horizontal position, then swing it back once over your head and toss it in a vertical position. That way, you stood less of a chance of catching more than one horse with it.

"Frank Blackburn, our wagon boss, was pretty good at catching horses out of the remuda. And so was I."

Once the Butcher Block cowboys were mounted, they would begin the day's work. Whether it was branding, castrating, doctoring or shipping, the first order of the day was to locate and bunch the cattle up, then move them to a general holding area where they could be worked.

"The horses we used to gather the cattle were called 'circle horses,' " Walter says. "We called them that because we would ride them in a huge circle—10 or 15 miles around—collecting the cattle and bringing them in. When we got the cattle to the holding area, we'd put the circle horses up for the day and switch to fresh mounts. All the work we did after that—the sorting and the roping—was done out in the open."

Somewhere near the middle of each working day, Walter and his fellow cowboys would break for lunch. It usually consisted of beef steaks or a beef roast, beans, potatoes and coffee.

After the noon break, it was back to working cattle. Though occasionally it would go on until dark, the workday generally ended around four or five p.m. The cowboys would ride back to the chuck wagon, put their horses up and settle in to wait for dinner. Like the noon meal, this usually consisted of beef, beans and coffee. Then the men would relax, sitting around the campfire until it was time to go to bed.

The nights were spent in bedrolls, under the stars. If it rained, which it seldom did, they slept under a tarp.

Although he was grateful for the $45 a month that Newcomb had started him out at, it was only a matter of months before Walter was able to improve his financial lot.

"I guess I'd been at the ranch for seven or eight months," he says, "when the cowboy who rode the rough string quit. I went to Frank Blackburn and told him I'd like to take the job on.

"The rough string was called that for a reason. There were usually around 15 horses in it, and they all had some sort of problem. They might be bad to buck, bite or kick. Anyone who rode the rough string was expected to do the same amount of work as all the other cowboys. It was just a little tougher to do it from the back of a spoiled horse.

"But the pay for the rough string rider was $75 a month and I wanted that money, so I took on the job. I rode those horses for two years and was even able to fix the problems on some of them and turn them back in with the regular remuda."

After the chuck wagon season was over, usually around the 15th of October, most of the Butcher Block cowboys were let go until the following spring. By the time Walter's first season with the crew was over, however, his boss had taken a big enough liking to him to keep him on.

"After that first year," Walter says, "Mr. Newcomb came to me and asked if I wanted to stay on with him and work the winter camp. I told him I sure would, and I spent three winters in a cabin with Dave Newcomb, his son.

"Our main responsibility was just to kind of prowl around through the cattle. In that country, we didn't feed a lot of hay. The cattle mostly just foraged for themselves. But there would be some that needed extra care. They might be sickly or just doing poorly, so we'd have to gather them up and feed them.

"We kept a string of six horses to work the cattle with," he continues. "And, like we did out on the range, we'd turn those horses out at night. But we kept a 'night horse' up in a corral. We'd use him to gather up the other horses each morning. Dave and I would take turns wrangling them.

"The second winter I spent in camp,

"I'm getting tired of riding these broncs. I just might go back to Oklahoma and try to raise some good horses."

the night horse we were using was bad to buck. It was my turn to bring the horses in, so I caught him up, saddled him and got on. He went to pitching and hit a spot of ice.

"He went down, fell on me and broke my ankle. I never went to the doctor, but I couldn't ride. So I just took over the cooking duties. Dave and I used to take turns at that, too, but after my accident, I handled the cooking for a solid month. I couldn't walk at all, but I could scoot around with my knee resting on a high-backed chair.

"After a month, the ankle healed to the point where I could start riding again."

For all its physical hardships and repetitiveness, to young Walter Merrick life as a cowboy came close to being ideal. And it was a lifestyle that he'd always wanted to be a part of and that would wind up standing him in good stead.

"I wouldn't trade the three years I worked for Mr. Newcomb for anything," he says. "I learned a lot about cattle and horses during those years. I learned how to handle them and how to evaluate them, how to pick apart their good and bad points.

"That was all knowledge that I'd been hungering to have ever since I was old enough to know what a cow and a horse was. And it was knowledge that I dreamed of putting to work some day to build something I

could call my own."

In the fall of 1928, after the last of the Butcher Block cattle had been shipped to market, C. P. Newcomb gathered his cowboys together one evening and told them that he would not be outfitting a chuck wagon the following spring—or any spring thereafter. He told his hands that they would all have to look for work elsewhere.

Most of the men took the news hard, but not Walter.

"After Mr. Newcomb broke the news to us," he says, "we all sat around that evening, talking about where we were going to go to look for work. Some of the boys talked about going to Wyoming, others to Nevada or Montana. I never said anything, and finally one of them asked me what I was going to do.

" 'I don't know,' I replied. 'I'm getting tired of riding these broncs. I just might go back to Oklahoma and try to raise some good horses.'

"Actually, I had already decided to do that," Walter says. "Mr. Newcomb had already indicated to me in private that he would be willing to keep me on the payroll, but my father's health had gotten steadily worse and he and my mother had moved back to Texola. I still felt like it was my responsibility to take care of them, so I said my goodbyes, loaded my saddle and bunk roll in the Model T car I had bought a short while earlier, and headed back south."

*The 1928 Butcher Block fall roundup marked the end of the ranch's chuckwagon era. After its completion, Walter Merrick returned to Oklahoma.*
**Photo courtesy Billie Fox**

# 3 PERFECT PARTNERS

*"The first time I laid eyes on Walt, I turned to my sisters and said,
'Don't you two even waste your time looking at that boy...he's mine.' "*
—Tien Merrick

THE WALTER Merrick who left Colorado in the fall of 1928 to return to Oklahoma was far different from the youngster who had migrated north seven years earlier.

Standing 6-feet, 4-inches tall with coal-black hair and piercing blue eyes, the lanky teenager might have still been an adolescent in calendar years but he was an adult in every other respect. Seasoned on the open range as both a ranch hand and a horseman, Walter was full of self-confidence and

optimism, and secure in the knowledge that he now had a viable trade to ply. In his mind, the only obstacle that lay ahead was landing a new job.

But times were getting tougher by the day in western Oklahoma. With the Dust Bowl days of the Great Depression looming just around the corner, gainful employment was becoming hard to find.

"To begin with, I almost had to walk the last few miles into Texola," Walter says. "I was almost there when the low gear went out on my Model T. In order to make it over the last few hills, I'd have to turn the car around, put it in reverse and back up to the top. Once I made it, I'd face the car in the right direction, pop it into second gear and take off. By the time I got home, I was wishing I'd brought a good saddle horse along."

Once he got settled in with his parents in Texola, Walter paid a visit to the owner of the ranch near which he'd been born.

"I rode out to the Davis Ranch on horseback and spent the night," he says, "Mr. Champion "Champ" Davis, one of the two brothers who owned the ranch, knew me from when I was a little kid. The next morning I asked him for a job.

" 'I'm just not hiring anybody,' he

*Champion "Champ" Davis, owner and manager of the Davis Ranch of Erick, Oklahoma, put 17-year-old Walter Merrick to work in 1929 as a horse breaker.*

**Photo courtesy Ed Davis**

said. 'We're out of money.'

" 'All right,' I said, "and we sat there and talked for a while. He knew I could ride and he finally said, 'I've got a lot of horses to break, so if you want to break them, I can pay you $10 a head, plus room and board.' I said, 'I'll take anything.' So he put me to work."

The next morning, Davis arranged for two cowboys to escort Walter to what was known as the "bronc pasture." There, the young rough stock rider found he had his work cut out for him.

"There were around 75 head in the bronc pasture," Walter says. "Some of them were like the horses I'd rode up in Colorado—spoiled or sour. But most of them just hadn't ever been broke to ride. They were from 3 to 11 years old, and hadn't been handled since they were caught up and gelded.

"Overall," Walter continues, "the Davis Ranch geldings weren't as high a quality of horseflesh as the Butcher Block Ranch stock. But a few of them were. On that first day, as I was cutting back some to start in on, I noticed a good-looking gray in the bunch. I asked one of the boys, 'What about this gray horse with the saddle marks on him?' He said, 'Oh, he's spoiled. Mr. Davis won't let you ride him. He won't let nobody ride him.'

"Let's cut him back," I said.

"So we cut him back and I snubbed him down, saddled him up and crawled on. And I'm here to tell you that horse did try me. But we got it worked out and came to an understanding. By the time it was all said and done, he made a whale of a ranch horse. His name was Blue Darter, and I rode him for years after that. There never was a job that I asked him to do that he didn't put his whole heart into."

Walter's initial task of rehabilitating and breaking 75 head of spoiled and untouched geldings for the Davis Ranch took him a full year to complete. His wages for the 12 months amounted to $750 in cold, hard cash, three square meals a day and a roof over his head at night. But it was work, and the young cowboy was grateful to get it. And at the end of the year, he'd made a strong enough impression on his boss to be offered a permanent position.

"After I had gone through all those geldings," Walter says, "Mr. Davis

*For the first several years that he worked for Champ Davis, Walter lived at the ranch headquarters.*

*As evidenced by this mid-1930s photo, the Davis Ranch Hereford cattle were considered some of the best in the Southwest.*

**Photo courtesy Ed Davis**

*Walter's initial task at the ranch was to break and gentle 75 head of riding geldings. The job took a full year and paid $750.*

to them and said, 'Don't you two even waste your time looking at that boy ... he's mine.' "

In many ways, the Davis Ranch that both Walter and Christien called home in 1928 was custom-made for in-house romance. For all intents and purposes, it was a small, self-contained community.

The ranch was formed in 1901 by two brothers—Champ and Edward T. Davis of Greer County, Territory of Oklahoma. Edward, the elder of the brothers, had been married, widowed and re-married by the time the ranch was acquired. Upon moving to the area with his second wife, he set up housekeeping in a home three miles north of the town of Erick. Champ, the younger brother, was a lifelong bachelor and lived on the ranch from the onset.

Originally comprised of 52 sections of land, or 33,280 acres, the Davis operation grew to encompass 65 sections, or 41,600 acres. In its heyday, the ranch raised cattle, horses, mules, sheep, goats, hogs, cotton, feed and alfalfa hay. At one time they also had a commercial fruit orchard.

The ranch maintained a commercial Hereford cow and calf operation of 4,000 mother cows and employed four or five cowboys to take care of them. In addition, roughly 20 farm hands were kept on the payroll to handle the agricultural chores.

All of the employees and their families were housed in 14-by-28-foot, two-room bungalows that were scattered throughout the property. A ranch church and schoolhouse provided for the residents' spiritual and educational needs.

For the first year that he was on the Davis Ranch payroll, Walter resided at the ranch headquarters. Christien, or "Tien" as she was nicknamed, lived with her family in one of the bungalows.

"Both my father, John Franklin Shinn, and my mother, Mary Estelle Meason, came from the Sweetwater, Texas, area," Tien says. "I was one of six girls in our family. Nina and the twins—Leslie and Layla—were older

offered me a full-time job as a cowboy. The pay was a dollar a day, or six dollars a week. The days were long and the work was hard, but I was doing what I loved and I never minded it at all."

Although he was unaware of it at the time, Champ Davis was not the only person that young Walter had made a favorable first impression on. For a certain farmer's daughter, the attraction was of a slightly different nature and one that she was determined to act upon.

"I'll never forget the first time I laid eyes on Walter," says Onna Christien Shinn Merrick. "I was just 15 years old at the time and was with a couple of my sisters. After I spied him, I turned

than me. Jean and Georgia were younger. For as far back as I can remember, I was the tomboy of the family. I always loved the outdoors and I always loved livestock. My dad used to say I was the only boy he ever raised."

Just as Walter and most of the other rural children of her generation had been, Tien learned the ways of hard manual labor at an early age.

"My dad was one of the Davis Ranch farm hands," she says. "He did whatever the ranch needed him to do in the way of farming. To help make ends meet, my mother and us girls would pick cotton. I learned to pick cotton long before I learned to read. In fact, I didn't even start school until the third grade. I started in the cotton fields before that.

"I've never stood more than five feet high or weighed more than 100 pounds, and I sure wasn't very big as a child. But it didn't take me long to realize that driving a team of work horses was a whole lot easier than picking cotton. By the time I was 10, I could handle a four-horse team and put in a full day's work with them.

"I used to need to stand on a big bucket to harness and unharness the horses, but that was still a lot easier than spending all day in a hot cotton field."

In the fall of 1928, Tien was 15 years old. A dark-complexioned, dark-haired, mere slip of a girl on one hand, on the other hand she was an energetic, young woman who knew exactly what wanted. And what she wanted was Walter Merrick.

"At different times, my dad and mom ran the cook shack for the Davis Ranch hands," Tien says. "I guess that's where I first saw Walter. But I still had to figure out a way to meet up with him and exchange a few words.

"One day I was driving a team of horses down a road, pulling a wagon. One of my sisters was with me and we saw Walter and one of the other cowboys off at a distance, riding toward us.

"I pulled the team up, jumped off

the wagon real quick and let the air out of one of the tires. My sister said, 'That's just too sneaky and underhanded for me. I'm going to tell that boy what you did.'

"I told her, 'You go right ahead. And while we're at it, let's just invite everyone else on the ranch and make it a real confessional. There's been a couple of stunts that you've pulled lately that I'm sure Mom would just love to hear about.'

"Why, you've never seen a girl clamp her mouth shut as quick as Sis did. Anyway, Walter rode up, stepped down off his horse and pumped up the tire. We visited a little bit and I was able to wrangle a date out of him, to go to the movies in Erick.

"Walter was a tall, bashful kind of guy to begin with, but that didn't matter to me. From the first time I ever saw him, I knew he was the one for me. I just had to convince him to feel the same way about me."

And Walter did get the message. After a courtship that lasted a year,

*Although this photo is blurred and hard to view, it shows 17-year-old Walter up on Blue Darter. Originally a soured ranch gelding, the gray was rehabilitated and placed back in the working remuda.*

he and Tien were married on October 6, 1930, by the Justice of the Peace in Erick.

"I knew that I wanted to marry Tien after about six months," Walter says. "But I wanted to wait until I was 19. So we did. My birthday was on October 5th, and we got married the very next day. You were supposed to be 21 to get married back then, so I just lied about my age. Tien was 16 by then, and her mom went with us and signed for her. We never took a honeymoon. We got married on a Sunday and went back to work on the ranch on Monday."

For the first several weeks of their marriage, the newlyweds lived in the Shinn household. Then, fortune smiled on them and one of the Davis Ranch farm hands quit. That freed up one of the bungalows and the newlyweds were quick to take up residence in it. Walter's father had passed away earlier that fall, so upon moving into their new home the couple brought Walter's mother out to the ranch to live with them.

Walter and Tien quickly settled into the routine of married life on the Davis Ranch. It was a life of hard work for both of them, with very few frills.

> "To tell you how smart we were, Tien and I got married right before the Depression hit."

"To tell you how smart we were," Walter says, "Tien and I got married right before the Depression hit. At that time, I was doing better than a lot of folks. I had even managed to sock away a little money in the bank in Erick.

"Right before the big stock market crash and mass bank closings of 1929, I happened to be in the bank one day. The bank president saw me and motioned for me to come with him back to his office at the rear of the building.

" 'Walter,' he said, 'how much money do you have in this bank?' 'Around $300,' I told him. 'I want you to come up front with me and draw it all out,' he said. 'I don't guess I want to do that,' I said. 'Walter, just do what I tell you,' he said. 'Draw it out and take it over to my brother's bank in Shamrock.'

"So I gave in and did as he told me. The next day, the bank in Erick closed its doors. A lot of folks lost their life's savings that day, but my money was safe in Shamrock. And I kept it there for years afterwards.

"Right after Tien and I got married, I traded in my Model T for a 1928 Chevy. I was drawing $45 a month in

*To earn extra money, Walter competed in the saddle bronc riding at local rodeos. Here, he makes a good ride at a 1929 contest.*

wages. As far as the farm hands went, Tien could handle a team of horses about as well as any of them, so she was drawing $1.50 a day in wages, too. We were getting by better than a lot of the folks around us.

"By this time," he continues, "my brother-in-law Curtis Willoughby and sister Ruby had also moved back from Colorado. Buck Couch came down with them, and he and Curtis went to work for the Davis Ranch.

"The cotton harvest started shortly after Tien and I got married, so she and Ruby went to work picking cotton—or pulling bolls they called it. The harvest lasted 60 days or so, and they got paid 50 cents for every hundred pounds they picked. They were both pretty fast and could pick 2,000 pounds a day between them. All things considered, we thought we were doing pretty well for ourselves.

"Mr. Davis was one of the best men I've ever had the privilege of knowing," Walter continues. "In some ways, he was just like a father to me.

"He was an old bachelor when I worked for him—never married—and he rode a horse everywhere he went. There weren't any cars, trucks or tractors anywhere on the ranch for most of the time I worked there. All the work was done with ranch or work horses.

"Mr. Davis didn't learn to drive a car until he was 65 or so. By that time he had developed some kidney problems and the doctor made him quit riding horses. He bought an old Model T Ford then, and it took him a year to learn to drive it. Even then he didn't drive too well. If he had a long trip to make, he usually took me with him to do the driving.

"But one thing about Mr. Davis," Walter continues, "he always took the welfare of his hired hands to be a personal responsibility. Money was tight in those days and getting tighter all the time, but Mr. Davis found other ways to compensate the people who worked for him.

"One of the things he would do was to allot 10 acres to each family and allow them to grow cotton on it. They

would supply the seed and the labor, but the money the harvested crop took in was theirs."

It was at this juncture of Merrick's life—in the fall of 1930—that the legend of the 14 Ranch was born, as was the brand that would go on to mark thousands of the top cattle and some of the most renowned Quarter Horses in the history of the West.

At the time of his passing, Walter's father had a modest life insurance policy. In it, he named his youngest child the sole beneficiary. The message to Walter could not have been clearer if it had been etched in stone.

*In the spring of 1936, Walter and Tien Merrick left the Davis Ranch and headed for Klamath Falls, Oregon, where they planned to buy a place of their own. Turned back by a Nevada blizzard, they touched down in Alamosa, Colorado.*

31

"I had been helping my folks get by for years," he says. "My father knew that I would be the one to take care of Mom after he was gone, so he had the insurance policy made out to me. After we buried him in the family plot just south of Erick and paid the funeral expenses, there was in the neighborhood of $750 left. I decided to put it to use the best way I knew how. I went out and bought some yearling calves, and Mr. Davis allowed me to run them on his range free of charge.

"Of course, I needed to brand them to set them apart from the Davis Ranch cattle. Several of the boys that worked with me came over one day to help me do it.

"As we gathered the calves and prepared to brand them, one of the boys said to me, 'Walter, what brand are you going to use on these calves?' 'I don't know,' I replied. And I didn't. I hadn't really given it much thought.

"Finally, I said, 'How many are there?' We counted them and there were 14. 'I guess that's our answer,' I said. 'Let's just slap a '14' brand on them and be done with it. And that's the brand I've used on my cattle and my horses ever since."

Life for the Merricks quickly settled into a tried-and-true, age-old pattern. Although he was never officially named ranch foreman, Walter's employer looked to him to take the lead in any and all matters having to do with the cattle and the horses. Walter received each day's marching orders from his boss, and then relayed them to the other cowboys. The work day generally began at daybreak and lasted until late afternoon. If the need arose, it was extended until dark. The work week was Monday through Saturday, with Sundays off.

At home in their two-room clapboard house, Tien and Fannie Merrick kept busy with housekeeping and cooking under the most primitive of conditions. Clothes were washed by hand using a scrub board and

*After securing work on the Howard Linger Ranch north of Alamosa, Walter and the rest of the Linger hands were dispatched to the mountains south of town to make the spring grazing pastures ready for occupation. A late snowstorm descended on the crew along the way.*

hung outside to dry, weather permitting.

None of the employee housing on the ranch came equipped with indoor plumbing or electrical power. Barrels held the water used for drinking and bathing. Outhouses, kerosene lamps, and wood- and coal-burning stoves were used. On occasion, an even more-basic fuel was taken advantage of.

"There was a cattle feed ground right next to that first house we lived in," Walter says. "I can still see Tien out there every day, picking up the dried cow chips. We burned them all that first winter. They didn't burn as long as wood or coal, but they burned every bit as hot and we were glad to have them."

As far as nutrition went, the Merrick family garden plot provided an array of vegetables, and dairy cows contributed milk, cream and butter. Chickens and hogs were an added source of meat and eggs. Beef, while readily available, was hard to preserve during the hottest three seasons of the year. Consumption of it was generally relegated to the winter months.

Life for the Merricks was harsh and stark by any measure, but it was what they had been born into and raised to endure. Far from being discouraged, they took a look around at the bankrupt families headed for the West Coast and considered themselves to be among the fortunate few.

As the "Dirty Thirties" progressed,

the Depression took a harsher hold on the land. Eking out an existence became even more of a struggle. The lack of appreciable rainfall turned the red dirt clay of western Oklahoma into a dustbowl. Cropland and garden plots became all but barren, and the price of cattle dipped so low that shipping them to processing centers in Kansas City or Omaha often realized little more than enough money to cover the freight.

In desperation, Champ Davis assembled Walter and all of the rest of his employees and presented them the only option he had to offer.

"It must have been in 1932 or 1933 that Mr. Davis called us all in," Walter says. "I can still remember exactly how he explained it.

"'Boys, I've run out of money,' he said. 'Now, I don't want to let anyone go, but I just can't afford to pay you as much as I have been. I don't expect you to like it, and I won't blame any man who wants to draw what he's got coming and pack up and leave. But I'm going to have to cut everybody's pay.'

"Mr. Davis cut our wages from $1.50 a day to $1.00 a day, but, to a man we stayed put. Where else were we going to go? There was no work anywhere. So we just went about our business, tightened our belts a little and made do with less.

And life went on much as before.

On June 19, 1933, Jimmie Wayne

"Boys, I've run out of money. Now, I don't want to let anyone go, but I just can't afford to pay you as much as I have been."

*With no access roads available, the crew was forced to pack much of their eating, sleeping and fencing supplies in.*

Merrick, Walter and Tien's first child, was born at home with the local doctor in attendance. With the young couple and their newborn son now occupying the rear portion of the house, and Walter's mother sleeping on a cot next to the kitchen stove, things were beginning to get a little cramped. Walter began once more to dream of greener pastures.

"During the winter of 1935–36," he says, "I began reading about railroad-owned land in Klamath Falls, Oregon, that was being sold cheap. Like most other folks, Tien and I had gotten a little leery of banks. We'd seen too many people lose everything they had when they woke up one morning to find bank doors closed and bolted.

"But we had still managed to increase our savings a little. Although we continued banking some in Shamrock, we kept most of it squirreled away at home. By the spring of that year I was inclined to

strike out for Oregon to buy a ranch. Dating back to when I had started working for the Butcher Block in Colorado, having a ranch of my own was what I dreamed about.

"Tien was always an adventurous soul, too. If I'd have said I thought we should move to Alaska and pan for gold, I believe she would have just started packing."

In early spring of 1936, Walter and Tien sold most of their cattle and possessions and moved Fannie Merrick in with Curtis and Ruby Willoughby. After trading their 1928 Chevy car in for a new GMC pickup, they loaded 3-year-old Jimmy and the few possessions that they had chosen to hold on to, and headed west.

As fate would have it, they would be back on the Davis Ranch in less than a year.

"We never made it all the way to Oregon," Walter says. "At Winnemuca, Nevada, we got caught

*Once the base camp was established, snow notwithstanding it was relatively comfortable and well-suited to the cowboys' needs.*

in a late-spring blizzard. The roads north and west were plugged tight, and it didn't look like they were going to be opened up any time soon.

"So we turned back. We backtracked to Monte Vista, Colorado, found some lodging, and I began to inquire about work. Howard K. Linger, who went on to become the Executive Director of the AQHA, had a big ranch north of Alamosa, near the little town of Hooper. I wound up going to work for him there."

Among the first chores Walter was tasked to complete on the Linger Ranch was traveling up into the high country southwest of Alamosa in the company of four other men and a string of pack horses. Once there, the men spent several weeks checking and repairing fences.

Shortly thereafter, a trainload of 2,000 steers were transported up the mountain via the narrow-gauge railway that ran from Alamosa to Chama, New Mexico. Upon arriving at their destination, the cattle were turned loose to graze.

Once again, Walter Merrick found himself a Colorado cowboy, caring for cattle out on the range. As always, it was a life that suited him. At least parts of it did.

"We didn't stay too long in Colorado," he says. "The work was what I was used to, and Mr. Linger had some nice ranch horses. Most of his stock had good remount Thoroughbred breeding behind them, and they were well-suited for use in and around the mountains.

"But, with all the mountains and trees, the country was a little closed-in for my liking. And it seemed like spring was awful slow in coming to that high country. And Tien started in missing her family. So, that fall we just loaded up and headed back to Oklahoma."

In any person's journey down life's road, there are crossroads where a step in one direction or the other can lead to altogether different destinations. The Nevada blizzard that prevented Walter and Tien from reaching their original goal was just

*Here's Walter at rest in camp on the Linger grazing grounds.*

such a crossroads. Had the storm never occurred, Walter might have proceeded on to the Northwest and lived out his life on an Oregon cattle ranch. As it was, he turned back to meet his true destiny.

It was a destiny that would see him set his saddle onto the back of a breed of horse that was undisputedly the fastest in the world. The ensuing ride would be a long and exciting one, and one that would take both man and horse to new and theretofore unheard of heights.

From the back roads and brush tracks of Oklahoma and Texas to the winner's circle of the All-American Futurity and beyond—from that day forward Walter Merrick's fate was sealed.

He was destined to become the dean of the Quarter racehorse men.

# 4 CRADLE OF SPEED

*... A quarter million people made the four runs for homes in Oklahoma...they came with the best horses it was possible to possess. Most of those horses stayed in Oklahoma."*
*—Franklin Reynolds*

JUST AS Walter Merrick was a product of that part of the West into which he was born, so, too, were the horses that would soon become an integral part of his life.

As was pointed out by author Franklin Reynolds in his two-part article, "Cradle of the Modern Quarter Horse," that appeared in the March and April 1957 issues of *The Quarter Horse Journal*, the horses that were popular in western Oklahoma at the time of Walter's birth and upbringing carried in their veins a legacy of speed. It was a heritage that had its roots in four of the greatest horse races ever held.

Those races were known as the Oklahoma Land Runs.

Between April of 1889 and September of 1893, close to 4½ million acres of Indian land in the Oklahoma Territory were opened up to white settlement. More than 250,000 aspiring land owners participated in the four "land runs" staged to mete out the acreage.

The rules were simple. The aspirants were assembled at a designated starting line. A gun was sounded and off they raced. The first to arrive at any given location owned it.

In an attempt to circumvent the rules of the contest, some aspiring

*From the mid-1800s on, Cheyenne, Oklahoma, was a hotbed of Quarter Horse activity. The livery barn shown at the far left in this early 1900s photo was probably the home of legendary sire Peter McCue.*

**Photo courtesy Judy Tracy**

# Peter McCue, Wt. 1430

**WILL MAKE THE SEASON OF 1911 AT CHEYENNE, OKLAHOMA.**

TERMS: $25 to insure colt to stand and suck. Pasture will be furnished for mares coming from a distance at $2 per month per head. Extra fine mares will be given special attention, and if desired will be kept in stable, a reasonable fee will be charged for keeping. Notes are to be signed when mares are bred or taken away. Care will be taken to avoid accidents, but will not be responsible should any occur. "Peter McCue" one of the greatest Quarter horses ever to run on a short track. His blood is found today in all quarter horses of note. While in St. Louis he ran the fastest quarter mile ever run by a horse on four legs, when he was clocked at 21 seconds flat.

TOM CAUDILL, Keeper

MILO BURLINGAME, Owner
Cheyenne, Oklahoma.

*As this reprint of a flier advertising Peter McCue shows, stud fees and mare board were a bit more reasonable in 1911.*

*After his arrival in Cheyenn in 1911, Peter McCue stood under the management of well known local horseman Tom Caudill. Evident in this shot is the left ankle injury that ended the famed stallion's racing career.*

landowners attempted to settle on the government land ahead of time. They were known as "sooners" and were evicted whenever and wherever they could be ferreted out.

Most runners resorted to the more-legal maneuver of stacking the deck in their favor by hitting the starting lines atop the best and fastest horses that they could acquire. Included among these mounts were Kentucky Whips, Thoroughbreds, Standardbreds and Saddlebreds.

Speed was not only a source of pride to these men and women, but a ticket to a new future, as well. After the land was settled, most of the horses stayed. Intermingled with native Western strains and infused with yet additional warm blood from the East and South, they produced a strain of horses the likes of which the West had never seen.

Cheyenne, Oklahoma, a wild and woolly Western town located in Roger

Mills County, 25 miles northwest of Erick, was especially rich in speedy stock. Other than fast horses, Cheyenne's greatest claim to fame stemmed from the fact that it lay just a few miles east of the "Washita Battlefield." There, at daybreak on November 27, 1868, General George Armstrong Custer and his 7th cavalry attacked and slaughtered a sleeping village of peaceful Cheyenne Indians under the leadership of Chief Black Kettle.

On April 19, 1892—just 24 years after the Washita Massacre— the Cheyenne and Arapaho country located in what is now western Oklahoma was opened to settlement via a land run.

Twenty-five thousand people participated in this contest, but for the first time in territorial history, there was more land than there were claimants for it. For the next decade, almost 2 million acres remained as open range.

*In these two photos taken in Cheyenne in 1911, the sons and daughters of Peter McCue are paraded down Main Street and posed together during the Roger Mills County Fair. That's Peter McCue in the background of the bottom photo.*

**Photos courtesy American Quarter Horse Heritage Center & Museum, Amarillo, Texas**

The most significant horseman to appear on the scene at this juncture was Sam Force. Traveling up from south Texas to make the run, Force brought with him his family and a band of 30 Steel Dust and Copper Bottom horses. Steel Dust was the first legendary foundation sire of the Quarter Horse breed. Copper Bottom, who had been brought to Texas from Kentucky in 1839 by Sam Houston, was likewise the founder of a great family of early-day Quarter Horses.

The Force horses were, in all probability, the first noted progenitors of the Quarter Horse breed to take up residence in the Cheyenne area.

Another noteworthy influx of speedy Steel Dust blood was brought to the area by two brothers—Phillip and Frank Trammel—who had begun

running cattle and horses in the area several years prior to the run. By blood or marriage, the Trammel brothers were part of the well-known Trammel and Newman families of Sweetwater, Texas.

Thomas Trammel, a third brother, established one of the first ranches in the Sweetwater area. By 1892, he was grazing 10,000 head of cattle on his Borden and Scurry County land, and was widely-known for the quality and speed of his horses. At one time or another, his horse breeding program was headed by such noted stallions as Black George and Rattler, both of whom were grandsons of Steel Dust; and Dan Tucker and Barney Owens, the sire and grandsire of Peter McCue.

Jim Newman, who married into the Trammel family, utilized the Trammel

*Eagle Chief, a 1942 sorrel stallion by Chief P-5 and out of Dee Waggoner, is a classic example of the Cheyenne country Peter McCue-bred Quarter Horse.*

**Photo courtesy American Quarter Horse Heritage Center & Museum, Amarillo, Texas**

blood and other early-day Steel Dust stallions such as Booger Red and Kid Weller, by Rancocas (TB), and Casey Jones and Ace, by Peter McCue.

Newman was also the breeder of Pan Zarita, a 1910 mare sired by Abe Frank (TB) and out of Caddie Griffith by Rancocas. Raced in the United States, Canada and New Mexico, and at one-time the holder of the world's record for five furlongs, Pan Zarita went to the post 151 times. Credited with 76 wins, 31 seconds and 21 thirds, she also met and defeated the highly-regarded Joe Blair—the sire of Joe Reed P-3—in a 3½ furlong match race held on February 5, 1916, in Juarez, Chihuahua, Mexico.

Due to the strong connection between Tom Trammel and Jim Newman in the Sweetwater area, and Frank and Phillip Trammel in the Cheyenne area, countless top horses of Trammel-Newman breeding made their way north, where they would go on to have a positive influence.

Although he was not from the immediate vicinity, pioneer horse breeder Charles B. Campbell of Minco, Oklahoma, also had a profound effect on the horses of the Cheyenne area.

Beginning in the late 1880s and lasting until the early 1920s, Campbell's cattle and horse ranching concerns were among the largest in the history of the state. At one time, he was reputed to have every acre of the Caddo and Chickasaw Indian Nation under lease.

Among Campbell's most noteworthy stallions were Pid Hart, a top racehorse and a full brother to Eureka, the sire of Old Joe Bailey; Bonnie Joe (TB), the sire of Joe Blair (TB); and Uncle Jimmy Gray (TB), by Bonnie Joe, another top runner and a great sire of early speed in the 1920s, 1930s and 1940s.

C.B. Campbell also bred Useeit (TB), the dam of two famous full brothers—Black Gold (TB) and Beggar Boy (TB). Black Gold was the 1924 Kentucky Derby winner, and Beggar Boy was a top sire of rodeo mounts and straightaway racers for Ronald Mason of Nowata, Oklahoma.

It is interesting to note here that Bonnie Joe, Uncle Jimmy Gray, Black Gold and Beggar Boy, though registered as Thoroughbreds, were all reputed to have carried early-day Quarter Horse blood.

Campbell's influence upon the horses of the Cheyenne area was the result of three young horsemen who went to work for him in 1890.

Dan and Reed Armstrong, who hailed from Kansas, were smallish in stature and excellent hands when it came to breaking and riding racehorses. Soon after they arrived on the scene, they were joined by a third brother named Johnnie.

The Armstrong brothers worked for Campbell for six years. Reed eventually married the daughter of Jake Meek, a local oxen-powered freight line owner and former buffalo hunter. In 1896, the Armstrong brothers and Meek all decided to pull up stakes and move to Elk City, a booming town located 28 miles southeast of Cheyenne.

In appreciation for their years of labor on his behalf, C. B. Campbell gave the quartet a string of top horses. Included among them were the stallions Pid Hart, Bob Peters, Tom Campbell and Ned Hanger; Nellie Heart, a Pid Hart daughter carrying the top race mare Catch Me in utero; Pickpocket, a gray racing gelding by Tom Campbell; several additional well-bred broodmares; and a number of young racing prospects.

All in all, it was one of the best bloodstock packages that could have been assembled at the time, and its impact on the horses around Cheyenne would be profound.

Cub Roberts and his daughter and son-in-law, Kizzie and Clyde McLean, who hailed from Leedy, Oklahoma, were yet another trio of horse breeders to bequeath the area with top seed stock.

Jeff C., an 1885 C. B. Campbell-bred gray stallion by Printer by Old Cold Deck and out of a Campbell mare, was one of Cub Roberts' better-known horses. He was a great racehorse in his own right and a noted sire of speed.

**Standing for a fee of $25, with a live foal guarantee, Peter McCue was heavily bred to the area's best mares.**

*Here's a never-before-published photo of A. D. Reed, one of the best-looking sons of Peter McCue. Bred by A. D. Hurley of Canute, Oklahoma, the 1916 bay stallion was out of Good Enough by Ned Harper. "Jock" Harrell is up in this circa 1917 or 1918 shot.*

**Photo courtesy J. W. Chalfant**

Joy, a 1912 sorrel stallion by Jeff C. and out of Lou Trammell by Peter McCue, was the McLeans' most noteworthy breeding animal.

In 1906 or 1907, the most legendary of all the early-day sires to impact the Cheyenne area made his appearance. This was Peter McCue, purchased from John Wilkins of San Antonio, Texas, by Milo Burlingame of Cheyenne for $10,000—a small fortune at the time.

Burlingame, who had ridden Peter McCue to some of his most impressive racing victories in St. Louis, Missouri, in 1897, was reputed to have received financial backing from a number of local horsemen—the Trammell brothers among them—in his quest to import Peter McCue to the area.

Once on the scene in Cheyenne, the ex-race champion was placed in the hands of Tom Caudill, a local livery

stable owner and top horseman. Standing for a fee of $25, with a live foal guarantee, Peter McCue was heavily bred to the area's best mares.

Included among those mares were daughters of Pid Hart, Casey Jones, Jeff C., Joy, Tom Campbell, Old Bob Peters, Young Bob Peters and Ned Hanger, as well as descendants of Steel Dust, Shiloh, Copper Bottom, Barney Owens, Dan Tucker and Cold Deck.

The resulting first-, second- and third-generation male descendants were some of the greatest ever attributed to Peter McCue during his long and illustrious breeding career. Included among them were John Wilkins (also known as John Wilkes), A. D. Reed, Badger, Chief P-5, Red Fish, Midnight, Whiskaway P-16, Dr. Blue Eyes, Billy the Tough, Jeff Self, Duck Hunter and Jack Dempsey.

Peter McCue left the Cheyenne area

in 1916, when he was purchased for $5,000 as a 21-year-old by Si Dawson of Hayden, Colorado. Utilized for the next seven years by Dawson and his famous neighbor Coke Roberds, the fountainhead sire continued to embellish his already shining reputation by siring such stellar performers and breeding animals as Buck Thomas, Sheik P-11, Squaw H. and Mary McCue—all of whom were out of daughters of Coke Roberds' famed sire, Old Fred.

Back in Oklahoma, the stage was set for the last piece of the early-day Cheyenne country speed horse puzzle to be put in place. That event occurred in 1927, when a 10-year-old boy named Kenneth "Skip" Montgomery showed up at the Frank and Gus Trammell Ranch near Elk City and very seriously informed the two older men that he wanted to become a breeder of fine horses.

Like his eventual friend and partner, Walter Merrick, Skip Montgomery had been raised during hard times and forced to grow up fast. Born in Allison, Texas, on January 1, 1917, he was one of 12 children who his mother was forced to raise alone after being abandoned by her husband.

The Montgomery boys, particularly Skip and his older brother Lindsey, developed into hard-working, promising horsemen at an early age. But whereas Lindsey was more interested in the rodeo and trading aspects of the game, Skip was intrigued by the breeding end.

The result of his youthful sojourn to the Armstrong Ranch was nothing less than astonishing. He so impressed both father and son with his early maturity and firm resolve that they gave him three well-bred mares as a gift. Betsy, the eldest of the trio, was sired by Kid Weller. Poor Mama, the next-oldest, was a daughter of Joy by Jeff C. But the choice mare of the package was Peachie, a yearling sorrel filly by Joy and out of Perfect Doll by Pid Hart.

Prior to visiting the Trammells, Skip had done some serious traveling around the countryside, visiting older horsemen and stallion owners, and making arrangements with them to breed his mares, when and if he ever got any.

Immediately after receiving the Armstrong mares, he took Betsy to the court of A.D. Reed, a 1916 bay stallion sired by Peter McCue and out of Good

*Among the top horses sired by A. D. Reed was Whiskaway P-16. Bred by E. A. Meek of Foss, Oklahoma, the 1924 sorrel stallion was out of Snip by Speedy Ball.*
**Photo courtesy American Quarter Horse Heritage Center & Museum, Amarillo, Texas**

*Billy The Tough, a 1927 sorrel stallion by A. D. Reed and out of Betsy by Kid Weller, was bred by Kenneth "Skip" Montgomery of Reydon, Oklahoma. Gelded before his true worth as a sire was realized, the stallion nevertheless exerted a tremendous influence on the Walter Merrick breeding program.*

**Photo courtesy J. W. Chalfant**

Enuf by Tom Campbell. A top racehorse who ran on the Thoroughbred tracks under the name of Dr. B. H., A.D. Reed was bred by A. D. Hurley of Foss, Oklahoma, and owned by John Harrel of Canute at the time Skip took Betsy to visit him. A sorrel colt named Billy the Tough resulted from this cross.

Of the three mares, Poor Mama had the least impact. Bred to Jeff Self by A. D. Reed in 1929, she foaled a brown stallion named Cimarron in 1930. Skip sold him to Aubra Bowers of Allison, Texas, and although the stallion was an above-average individual, Bowers promptly gelded him.

Peaches, the youngest of the gift horses, was the one slated to have the most impact on not only the Cheyenne country horses, but the entire Quarter Horse breed as well. Taken to the court of Midnight by Badger by Peter McCue in 1931, she foaled a typey chestnut filly named Salty in 1932.

At the time of her birth, Salty was the embodiment of the best of the Cheyenne country's heritage of speed. Her great grandsires were Peter McCue, Kid Weller, Jeff C. and Pid Hart—four of the greatest racehorses and speed sires to ever grace the area.

Unshown and unraced, Salty nevertheless went on to become one of the American Quarter Horse Association's first premier producers. All told, she was the dam of 14 foals. Four of them—Midnight Jr., Revenue, Salty Chief and Merrick's War Bond— would be acquired by Walter Merrick as part of his foundation herd.

They, and others of their ilk, were exactly the kind of horses that a man could use to build a breeding program rich in athletic ability and speed. And that's exactly what 25-year-old Walter Merrick, fresh from his short side trip to the north and west, was determined to do.

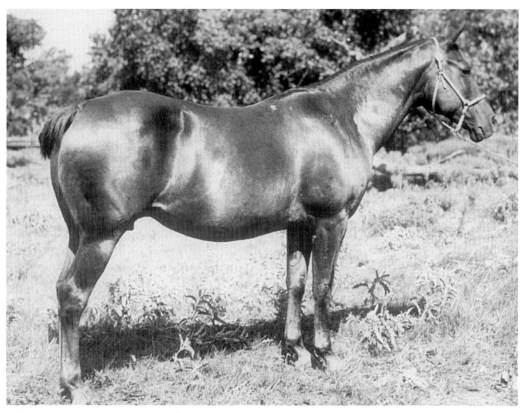

*Salty, a 1932 chestnut mare by Billy The Tough and out of Peachie by Joy, was the cornerstone matriarch of the Walter Merrick Quarter Horse program. Although he never owned her, Walter did eventually acquire three of her sons and one of her daughters.*
**Photo courtesy American Quarter Horse Heritage Center & Museum, Amarillo, Texas**

# 5 A SOUND FOUNDATION

*"I never saw Peter McCue or A. D. Reed, but I saw a lot of their offspring and I knew they were the kind of horses I wanted to raise."*
—Walter Merrick

WALTER AND Tien Merrick arrived home in western Oklahoma in the fall of 1936. Upon learning that his top hand had returned, Champ Davis was more than agreeable to giving Walter his old job back.

Once re-settled on the Davis Ranch, life for the Merricks proceeded in much the same manner as it had prior

*Several years after returning to Oklahoma and the Davis Ranch, Walter purchased 320 adjoining acres and moved his family onto it. The homestead was a 16-by-32 foot structure, built into the side of a hill. Here are 7-year-old Jimmie and 1-year-old Donna Merrick, photographed in 1940 in front of the dugout.*

to their eight-month excursion. There were two notable exceptions, however.

Walter now had two goals firmly in mind. The first—a carryover from his days as a Butcher Block cowboy—was to own and breed some good horses. The second was to have a ranch of his own to put them on.

"By this time," Walter says, "I had started competing in rodeos, in the bronc riding and calf roping. Because of my job, I couldn't travel very far. No more than 50 or 100 miles in any direction.

"I wasn't a world champion-caliber cowboy, but I could usually hang in there enough to get my entry fees back and a little to boot. I also got to travel to some different parts of the country, meet some new people, and see what kind of stock they were riding.

"Mr. Davis subscribed to a livestock magazine called The Cattleman. It came out of Fort Worth, and every month they had a feature on an outstanding Quarter Horse. I'd borrow those magazines and study up on horses and bloodlines.

"I knew there were a lot of good horses in the Cheyenne country. Both Joe Reed P-3 and Chief P-5 were there. They were nice horses, and so were some of their offspring. But they didn't plumb suit me.

"I never saw Peter McCue or A. D.

Reed, but I saw a lot of their get, and I knew they were the kind of horses I wanted to raise."

In the course of attending rodeos around the country, Walter began to conduct an earnest search for a stallion to head up his program.

"I knew the Montgomery boys from over east of Elk City," he said. "Lindsey was a top calf roper and I'd see him at some of the rodeos. Skip was around a lot, too, so I got well-acquainted with him, as well.

"I also knew about the mares Skip had talked Frank and Gus Trammel out of. I'd seen the Salty mare, and I'd seen her sire, Billy The Tough. They were two of the best horses in this area at the time.

"So, I kind of started paying more attention to the Montgomery program, hoping a horse would come along that would show some potential as a stud."

At different times during their teens and early 20s, both Lindsey and Skip had worked for Aubra Bowers, a former JA Ranch cowboy who owned an 11-section spread near Allison, Texas.

Shortly after leaving the JA Ranch, Bowers had returned to purchase their famous old sire, Midnight. A 1916 gray stallion by Badger by Peter McCue, and out of Nellie Trammell by Pid Hart, Midnight had been bred by Jess Cooper of Roosevelt, Oklahoma.

After a short but brilliant racing career, Midnight went on to gain considerable fame as a herd sire for both the W. T. Waggoner Ranch of Vernon, Texas, and the JA Ranch. Among his most famous get were the three foundation Quarter Horse sires, Chubby, (One-Eyed) Waggoner and Rainy Day.

As noted earlier, the then-teenaged Skip Montgomery bred Salty to the then-20-year-old Midnight in 1936.

Midnight passed away a few short months after covering Salty, and her foal by him was destined to be his last. Born June 5, 1937, and coal black in color, he was named Midnight Jr.

In the summer of 1938, Skip headed for the West Coast in search of employment. He left his small band of

Quarter Horses in the care of his older brother. It proved to be a costly error.

"Lindsey Montgomery was a trader," Walter Merrick says. "He'd trade about anything he had if you caught him right. I had heard about Skip's Midnight colt, so I went over to the Montgomery place in the fall of 1938 to look him over.

"I liked him a lot and offered Lindsey $300 on the spot for him. That was a pretty stout price to give for a yearling colt in those days, and Lindsey agreed to sell. I had to borrow the money from the bank in Shamrock to do it.

*Here's Walter, Tien and Jimmie, circa 1936, at home on the Davis Ranch during the height of the Great Depression's "dust bowl" days.*

"After I asked the bank president for the loan and told him what it was for, he said to me, 'Walter, that's an awful lot of money to be giving for a horse. But I guess you know what you're doing, so I'll go ahead and loan you the money.' "

From the standpoint of breeding, Walter's new acquisition was exactly what he'd been searching for. Midnight Jr.'s sire was a grandson of Peter McCue on the top, and Pid Hart on the bottom. Salty, as mentioned earlier, was also Peter McCue and Pid Hart-bred, with Jeff C. and Kid Weller thrown in for good measure.

Conformation-wise, Midnight Jr. also suited Merrick. Good-headed and necked, with ample bone and muscling, he matured to stand 14-3 hands high and weigh 1,100 pounds.

With his future herd sire in hand, next on Walter's agenda was to build up a small, select broodmare band and acquire a ranch of his own. As luck would have it, the opportunity to buy the ranch presented itself first.

"In the spring of 1939," Walter says, "a half-section of nearby land that was located around five miles north and east of the Davis Ranch headquarters came up for sale.

"It was owned by an elderly gentleman named Jim Walker. He was about the same age as Champ Davis and had gone to work for the Davis Ranch when it was first founded. At some point, he got some money together and bought that land and built a dugout house to live in, and some barns and corrals.

"I bought the half-section from him, and later bought the adjoining half-section from another man. I gave Mr. Walker $50 an acre for his land. I bought the other half of the section from a bank in a foreclosure kind of deal. It wasn't as good as the first half, and I didn't have to give as much for it.

"The whole piece was known as the Salt Grass section. The dugout was built into the side of a hill that overlooked a marshy area. That ground was made up of mostly alkali soil and that's where the salt grass part came in, because it thrived in that low area. It was a good ranch, with a creek that ran all the way through it, and I moved my family and my livestock over there pretty quick."

All the while he was searching for a ranch to buy, Walter was continuing to look for mares of just the right

**"I was on the lookout for some mares with A. D. Reed and Billy The Tough breeding."**

*In 1938, Walter purchased the yearling Quarter Horse stallion Midnight Jr. P-210 for the unheard-of price of $300.*

breeding and type to start his Quarter Horse breeding program.

The first broodmare that he found was one of the only two Billy The Tough daughters in existence. This was Grey Annie, a 1932 gray mare out of a mare by Casey Jones by Peter McCue.

"I was on the lookout for some mares with A. D. Reed and Billy The Tough breeding," Walter says. "By this time, the Montgomery boys had traded 'Billy' to Gus Armstrong. The stud had only sired maybe four or five foals, but he had a reputation for being ill-tempered and bad to buck. Shortly after Gus got him, he gelded him.

"I don't know anything about the temperament part, but from what Skip told me later, the bucking part came because he was taught to do it.

"Those Montgomery boys had started saddling him up when he was a late yearling. They'd put a flank strap on him and buck him out, just like I did the wild horses when I was a kid back in Trinchera. It kind of backfired on them, though, because when they went to gentle him out as a 2-year-old, he'd still try to buck 'em off.

*Shortly after acquiring Midnight Jr., Walter began assembling a broodmare band. Among his first significant purchases were the Peter McCue-bred mares Grey Annie (left) and Polly Reed (third from left). The remaining two mares in this shot were owned by the Davis Ranch.*

*In this second shot of the original Merrick mares, Polly Reed is on the far left and Grey Annie is on the right.*

*Golden Wolf, a 1932 sorrel mare by A. D. Reed by Peter McCue, was another of Walter's five foundation mares.*

"Lindsey did get him broke enough to rope calves off of, though, and a fellow named Elmer Cress over in Allison even borrowed him and raced him a little. But I don't think anyone ever got the horse plumb over that bucking.

"When I first saw Billy The Tough," Walter continues, "I thought he was about the best horse I'd ever laid eyes on up to that time."

"Anyway, Grey Annie was a direct daughter of Billy The Tough, and a good one to boot. I bought her from a man up around Reydon," Walter says. "He was a farmer, but he was almost blind at the time, so he wasn't doing much of anything with her. He just kept her in a little corral by the house.

"After Annie, I was able to locate and purchase two direct daughters of A. D. Reed.

"Polly Reed, the older of the two, was a nice-looking, blaze-faced sorrel mare. She had been bred by Fad Hill of Sunray, Texas, and was foaled in 1927.

I never was able to determine how her mother was bred.

"The other mare, Golden Wolf, was probably the best-built mare that I started my band with. She was bred on the Baca Ranch in Gallegos, New Mexico, and carried their brand. I bought her from a farmer named Tom Willey, who lived near Willow, a little community 30 miles southeast of Erick. When I first laid eyes on Golden Wolf, she was part of a four-horse team that was pulling a two-row lister. I think I gave $75 for her."

In addition to Grey Annie, Polly Reed and Golden Wolf, Walter purchased two additional mares of A. D. Reed breeding. Along with Midnight Jr., they were the foundation of his breeding program.

In 1940, with a small ranch and a select group of Quarter seedstock in his possession, 29-year-old Walter Merrick was now ready to tackle the next stage of his life.

To begin with, while not the lap of luxury by any stretch of the imagination, dugout life was a step up for the Merrick family.

"The sides of the dugout were made up of poured concrete," Walter says. "Mr. Walker hadn't been too exacting when he built the forms and poured the concrete. It had spread out at the bottom and come out over the forms in places.

"Still, the house was considerably bigger than the one we'd just vacated. It had two rooms that were about 16-by-16 feet, and it also had a 12-by-12 foot roofed entryway that led down a few steps to the main part of the house. So we'd gone from around 400 square feet of living space in the Davis Ranch bungalow to over 650 square feet in our new home. That seemed like a pretty big jump to us."

Like their previous home, the Merricks' new one did not come equipped with indoor plumbing or electricity. Drinking and bathing water was, if anything, harder to get. For the most part, it was hauled from a Davis Ranch windmill pump located five miles away, and stored in a rain barrel at the side of the house.

However, there was one notable improvement, instituted by Walter, that provided the family with their first taste of in-house entertainment.

"Shortly after we moved into the dugout," Walter says, "I built a wind generator tower right next to the house. It wasn't powerful enough to generate much electricity, but there was enough to power an old Philco crystal radio that we'd bought.

"We'd sit around in the evenings, listening to that radio for an hour or two before we went to bed. Our favorite program was W. Leo Daniels and the Light Crust Dough Boys. They came out of Fort Worth every night around 7:30. They'd sing and play stringed instruments and advertise Light Crust flour. We sure enjoyed 'em."

On October 22, 1939, Donna Margaret Merrick, the couple's second child, was born at the hospital in Shamrock. According to Walter, his eldest daughter almost came into the world in the front seat of the family car.

"The day Donna was born," he says, "I had gone to Wheeler to take delivery on a brand new Chevy car. When I got back home, Tien's labor pains were coming so close together that I knew I had to get her to the hospital.

"We all piled into the car and headed west toward Shamrock. It was about a 20-mile drive and I didn't want to drive too fast. In those days, you had to baby a new car along for the first 1,000 miles or else you stood a good chance of tearing the engine up.

"I drove as fast as I thought I could, and we just barely made it to the hospital in time. For a while there, I thought the baby was going to be born on the road."

Although he now found himself a landowner, Walter continued his role as Champ Davis's right-hand man. Every workday, he would rise before daybreak, take care of his own livestock, saddle up a ranch gelding and then ride to either the ranch headquarters or a pre-determined working location.

**The year 1940 marked the first crop of Midnight Jr. foals.**

*Discovered pulling a plow, Golden Wolf went on to become a race Register of Merit producer.*

*With an eye toward adding more speed and usability, Walter incorporated the blood of the legendary Joe Hancock into his early horse breeding program. The famous Peter McCue grandson is shown here with Lige Reed at the halter.*

**Photo by John Stryker**

In addition, by the end of 1939, Walter Merrick was a bona-fide cattle rancher and horse breeder.

Having moved in the neighborhood of 30 head of cattle—cows, calves and yearlings—from the Davis Ranch to the Saltgrass Section, Walter added another 120 head over the course of the next three years.

As another indication of the high esteem Champ Davis had for his young hand, the older rancher allowed Walter to have free use of some of his top registered Hereford bulls as range sires.

Relocating his young stallion, five mares, and two or three head of ranch geldings to his new holdings as well, the 28-year-old cowboy made his first breeding crosses and sat back to await the results.

The year 1940 marked the first crop of Midnight Jr. foals. From it came several noteworthy individuals, including General MacArthur, Sugar Foot M. and Clint Higgins.

General MacArthur, a Merrick-bred bay stallion out of Polly Reed, was sold as a yearling to George Mees of Corona, California.

Sugar Foot M., a Merrick-bred bay mare out of a mare of unknown breeding, was kept as a replacement filly and went on to become a top broodmare. Bred to Chigger M., a son of Midnight Jr., she produced a mare named Chigger's Baby. Chigger's Baby, when bred to Win Or Lose, produced all-time leading sire Sonny Dee Bar.

Clint Higgins, a black stallion out of Topsy by Jeff Self by A. D. Reed, came as a result of an outside breeding.

"Clint Higgins, the man, was a man from over by Wheeling who I had become well-acquainted with," Walter says. "The year that Midnight Jr. was a 2-year-old, Clint brought several nice mares over to breed to him.

"The best one was Topsy. She was a double-bred Peter McCue mare, and her colt, Clint Higgins, turned out to be a good show horse and a top sire."

In addition to being the year that Walter's first crop of Quarter Horse foals hit the ground, 1940 was significant in one other way. It was the time when the young horse breeder registered his first horses with a fledgling livestock registry known as the American Quarter Horse Association (AQHA).

"Through reading *The Cattleman* magazine," he says, "I knew there was a movement afoot to start up a Quarter Horse registry. As soon as I knew it had happened, I found out how to join up and request that my horses be inspected for registration.

"In late November of 1940, Mr. Jim

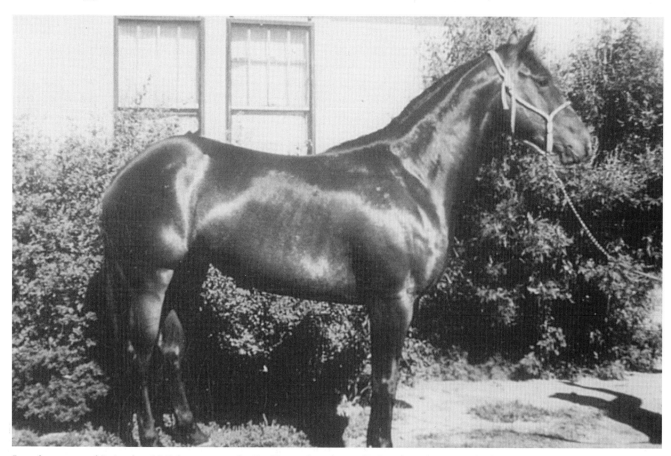

*Joan (pronounced JoAnn), a 1940 brown mare by Joe Hancock and out of Triangle Lady 1, was the first of the Burnett Ranch-bred fillies that Walter acquired.*

*In 1940, Walter purchased a second stallion to groom as a potential herd sire. Bred by Skip Montgomery, Salty Chief P-735 was a 1939 chestnut stallion by Chief P-5 and out of Salty. He is shown here with Walter at the New Mexico State Fair in Albuquerque.*

Minnick, the association's main inspector, came to my place. Mr. Minnick was one of the most-respected horsemen and judges in the country at the time. He was an ex-polo player, and he and I admired the same kind of horses.

"I'll never forget that day," Walter continues. "Mr. Minnick looked at Midnight Jr., the mares, and all the young stock. We visited a while, went in and had lunch, and then went back outside and looked at the horses some more.

"I could see Mr. Minnick was working up to something. Finally, he asked, 'What would you take for that black 2-year-old colt?' 'He's not for sale,' I said. 'I bought him to build a program around. If I sold him, I don't know where I'd go to get another one like him.'

"He studied on that for a while and then he said, 'Young man, I don't blame you for not pricing him. He's a fine horse, and I'll make a prediction. If you'll stay with the kind of animals that we've looked at here today, you'll go far in the horse business.'

"Those remarks sure made me feel good. They made me feel like I was headed in the right direction."

The year 1941 served to reinforce the optimism that Walter felt regarding his horse program and the direction it was headed. Grey Badger II, a gray stallion out of Grey Annie, was foaled that year. He would, as will be detailed in a subsequent chapter, go on to become one of the most legendary match racers to ever come out of the Cheyenne country.

It was also at this time that Walter, looking to increase the size of his broodmare band, made a trip south into Texas and established a relationship that would bear fruit for years to come.

"Through the rodeos," Walter says, "I had become acquainted with a Texas cowboy named Rex Keith. He managed the Triangle division of the Burnett Ranches, located at Paducah, Texas.

"In the fall of 1941, I paid a visit to the Burnett Ranch and bought a yearling filly who was probably the best individual I'd owned up to that time, and who grew up to be one of my best early-day producers.

"She was a brown filly, sired by Joe Hancock and out of Triangle Lady 1, by Mike Beach. We named her Jo Ann, after her sire and the lady who ramrodded the Burnett Ranch. Later, when we went to register her with the AQHA, that name was already taken so we registered her as Joan. But she was always Jo Ann to us."

Walter's visit to the Burnett Ranch opened the door to a lifelong friendship with Anne Burnett Tandy, or "Miss Anne," as she was more commonly called.

In the spring of 1942, accompanied by her husband and Rex Keith, the legendary Fort Worth scion and matriarch of the vast Burnett Ranch enterprises, paid her first visit to Walter's Oklahoma ranch.

Arriving in style in a brand new Cadillac, she was treated to her first glimpse at the young Oklahoma rancher who later became both a dear friend and advisor. In recalling the event in later years, Miss Anne would say, "We stopped the car in front of this little dugout built into the side of a hill. A man who was so tall he had to duck to get through the doorway came out. He was the best-looking damn cowboy I'd ever laid eyes on."

The official purpose of the visit was to look at a young Quarter Horse stallion that Walter had for sale.

"I was so satisfied with Midnight Jr.," Walter says, "that I went back to the Montgomerys in the fall of 1940 and bought his half-brother. He was a 1939 chestnut stallion by Chief P-5 and out of Salty.

"He was later registered as Salty Chief, and he grew up to be a fairly decent-looking horse. But I was partial to Midnight Jr. and I didn't see how I needed two studs, so I sold Salty Chief to Miss Anne when he was 3. He was the first of several studs that she bought from me."

As the friendship between the Texas baroness and Oklahoma cowboy deepened, it evolved to the point where Burnett would fly up in her private airplane, pick Walter up, and take him back to the Burnett Ranch to advise her on her horse breeding efforts.

"Miss Anne would bring me back to Texas," Walter says, "and ask me to help her sort her mares. She'd want to know which mares I thought should be put together with which studs.

"I enjoyed doing that, but I'd say to her, 'Miss Anne, you shouldn't have me doing this. You've got people here who've been making these decisions for years, and they're not going to take kindly to having someone like me come in and kind of take over.'

" 'I don't care,' she said. 'I value your eye for a horse and your judgment. If anyone gets bent out of shape over what you're doing for us, they'll just have to get over it.'

"Miss Anne and me stayed friends for a long time. Right up to the day she passed away, I guess. And she treated me well. She bought horses from me. I was able to go down there every fall and take my choice of those good Joe Hancock- and Roan Hancock-bred yearling fillies for $150 a round.

"It was a friendship that meant a lot to me, and one that I'll never forget."

At the same time he was building up and registering his Quarter Horse herd, and establishing an ever-broader base of friends and customers, Walter was also getting his first taste of a new kind of horse endeavor—match racing.

That he did so should have come as no surprise to anyone who knew either the man or the climate he lived in.

From the days of his childhood and forced early rise to maturity, Walter was a risk-taker by nature. He was a man who dared, a man who was always reaching higher and seeking more.

Western Oklahoma, with its rich heritage of daring men and women and fast horses, formed the perfect setting for anyone who had a little faith in himself and lady luck, and the desire to make a match.

And Walter Merrick was quick to seize the opportunities at hand.

**At the same time he was building up and registering his Quarter Horse herd, Walter was also getting his first taste of a new kind of horse endeavor— match racing.**

# 6

# TO MAKE
# A MATCH

*" 'I'm just a cowboy and I ain't got much money. If I lose
this horse race, I probably won't have enough to get home on.' "*
*—Walter Merrick*

*This classic photo of Walter Merrick and Midnight Jr., taken in 1940, tells quite a story. Behind the man and horse are the 1939 Chevy car and homemade horse trailer that transported them to rodeos and match races. Farther back stands a barrel reserved for drinking and bathing water, and behind it is the entrance to the Merrick's dugout home. Finally, behind the dugout entrance can be seen the wind generator used to power the family's crystal radio.*

ALTHOUGH WALTER Merrick's career as a racehorse man didn't officially begin until the late 1930s, its roots went much further back—back to the thrill of winning those first races he rode on Elmer Renner's gelding, Olin, when he was a kid in Texola.

Later on, as a cowboy on the Butcher Block Ranch in Colorado, he was exposed to organized racing.

"Mr. Newcomb, the owner of the Butcher Block, had some nice horses," Walter says. "His main stallion during the years I worked for him was a black, strip-faced, stocking-legged horse named Chief. I never knew his actual breeding, but I do know he came from the Coke Roberds Ranch in northern Colorado. And Coke was the man who had Peter McCue when he died. Chief's colts were above-average horses, and they had a little speed."

Once a year, the Butcher Block Ranch horses got a chance to test their racing mettle against all of the neighboring stock, in what was the biggest social event of the year.

"When I was working on the roundup wagon at the Butcher Block," Walter says, "we'd all get time off in September to go to the fair in Trinidad. All the ranchers and their cowboys would go to it. That would be the end of the branding season, and

each outfit would bring their chuck wagon and saddle horses to the fair. Mr. Newcomb alone would take in the neighborhood of 100 head.

"Horse racing was a popular event at the fair," he continues. "There was flat saddle racing, for both purses and matched money, and there was relay racing.

"In the purse- and match racing, I remember one horse in particular. He was a tall, leggy buckskin gelding with four stockings. His name was Yellow Gold, and he was pretty much a legend in that part of the country. I found out later that he was a Coke Roberds-bred horse, too, a grandson of Old Fred.

"In the relay races, the cowboys would have to ride four horses—once around the track with each of them. After completing each leg of the race, they'd jump off, switch their stock saddles to the next horse, and take off again.

"Mr. Newcomb's son, Dave, rode the Butcher Block relay string. I was a big, strong kid back then, so I'd usually be tagged as one of his holders. I'd hold a bareback horse in line, and keep holding him as Dave switched his saddle onto him. Then I'd turn him loose and off they'd go. Those were pretty exciting horse races, and the crowds seemed to really enjoy them."

*It was while breaking 2-year-old Midnight Jr. for use as a calf roping horse that Walter discovered the breakaway speed that made him feel the horse would make a match racer.*

*General MacArthur P-991 was the first Walter Merrick-bred horse to be registered with the AQHA. A 1941 bay stallion by Midnight Jr. and out of Polly Reed, he was sold as a yearling to George Mees of Corona, California.*

**Photos courtesy American Quarter Horse Heritage Center & Museum, Amarillo, Texas**

A decade after leaving southern Colorado and the Butcher Block Ranch behind, Walter found himself the owner of a 2-year-old black colt who turned his thoughts to racehorses once more.

"I broke Midnight Jr. in 1938, when he was 2," he says. "He was easy to break, and it wasn't long before I was trailing and roping calves off of him. He had such a tremendous burst of speed out of the box that I started taking him to rodeos and putting the word out that I'd like to match a race.

"There were some people from Durham, Oklahoma, by the name of Meeks—an older man and his two grown boys. They came down to my place and wanted to look at Midnight Jr.

"Most of the horses that were match racing in those days carried a little Thoroughbred blood and they showed it in their conformation. Midnight Jr. was a bulldog Quarter Horse—short and heavily muscled.

"Those fellas went into the box stall with him and I stayed outside. One boy's name was Edward. I heard the old man say, 'Edward, let's match him. He looks like a little draft horse.'

"So we set a date and I went up to Durham and ran against their horse for $300. Blue Cordin, a friend of mine from Tampa, went with me. Blue bet all the money he was carrying on the race, and I bet a little on the side, too.

"Those boys were eager to accommodate us. They just knew they were going to pick us clean. But Midnight Jr. beat their horse easy, and we just about broke them instead.

"That was in the fall of 1939, and that was the first race I ever matched."

For 28-year-old Walter and his 25-year-old wife, Tien, their first back road race victory hinted of a change in their lifestyle that was hard to comprehend.

*Here's another shot of Midnight Jr., taken in 1940 and this time with 7-year-old Jimmie Merrick in the saddle.*

Here they were, at the end of the Great Depression, living on six dollars a week in wages. All of a sudden, they take a horse to a Sunday match race and return with more than $300 in their pockets. It was easy money—almost too easy—and almost too good to be true.

To say the least, they were hooked.

"After the Durham race," says Walter, "I decided to get serious about Midnight Jr.'s training. I still had to get up every morning and go to work, but Tien didn't. And she had always been a good hand with a horse.

"We cleared off an oval track on some flat ground above the dugout, and every day Tien would get in the car and lead Midnight Jr. up there with her arm sticking out the window.

"She'd start out by leading him around the track from the car, at a trot. After he was warmed up a bit, she'd speed up so that he had to canter. At the end of the workout, she'd head back toward the barn. That's when the real horse race began.

"Midnight knew he was headed home, so he'd take off at a dead run. Tien would have to pedal pretty hard to keep up with him. As far as I know, she never let him get away. If she did, she never told me about it.

"That horse was pretty hard on the car, though. He'd get to feelin' good and kick the back fender of the car with his inside hind leg. It wasn't very long before he had that new car beat up pretty bad. But I didn't mind. Not with the kind of money he was making us."

For the remainder of 1938, Walter continued to haul Midnight Jr. to rodeos in Western Oklahoma and the Texas Panhandle. When he deemed the conditions right, he would scare up a match race. Both the times and the horse worked to his advantage.

"It was sure easier to match race a horse back then," Walter says. "To begin with, word didn't get around as quick then as it does now. I could match a race at one location, then show up at another one 50 or 100

*In September of 1941, Walter agreed to sell Midnight Jr. to H. S. Bissell of Las Cruces, New Mexico, for the heady price of $1,000 including delivery. Here are Walter, "Jr." and 2-year-old Donna on the day of their arrival in Las Cruces.*

miles away in a couple of weeks, and no one in the second place would have heard about the first race.

"And Midnight Jr. didn't look like a racehorse. He looked like a ranch horse and a rope horse. So people were always sure that their horse could beat him. But they never did. We finished out the year running maybe a half-dozen races, and we were never beat."

By the following year, however, word about Merrick's speedy stud had gotten around. In order to drum up any competition, the enterprising young rancher was forced to go farther and farther from home.

"By the middle of his 3-year-old year," Walter says, "I couldn't hardly match a race anywhere in the local area. But they had a nice rodeo every year down at Seymour, Texas, a little town located around 150 miles south of Erick.

"By this time, Skip Montgomery had developed into a pretty good jockey.

So, one day we loaded up Midnight Jr. and Cimarron, Skip's rope horse, and headed south. I had a half-ton Ford pickup with stock racks on the back, and we just hauled the stud and the gelding side-by-side in it. Midnight was trained to where he'd just jump into the back of that pickup from level ground.

"We made it down to Seymour and got entered up in the calf roping. As soon as we got settled, I put the word out that I was looking to match a race. It was a three-day rodeo, and, by the third day, nobody had mentioned a horse race.

"E. Paul Waggoner, the owner of the Waggoner 3D Ranch in Vernon, Texas, was there with his chuck wagon and cowboys. He finally came up to me and said, 'Young man, I hear you're looking to match a horse race.' 'Yes sir,' I said, 'I am.'

" 'What do you have for a racehorse, how far do you want to go, and how much do you want to run for?' he asked. 'I've got a little rope horse,' I said. 'I'll match him against any other rope horse here, at 300 yards, for a dollar a yard.'

"All the while we were talking, there was a Waggoner cowboy nearby, mounted on a nice-looking bay horse. 'I'll just match you, then,' Mr. Waggoner said. 'I'll run this bay horse against your black.'

"We piled into Mr. Waggoner's brand new Cadillac car and headed outside of town to try to find a level spot to run the race on. There was a bunch of his cronies in the car, and they were passing a whiskey bottle around, laughing and joking with me.

"They passed it to me, and I took a swig. The next time it came around, though, I just "lipped" it. I didn't swallow. I figured I needed to keep my wits about me.

"Those ol' boys started badgering me to bet more money. I said, 'I ain't got much money. I'm just a cowboy, and if I lose this horse race, I probably won't have money enough to get home on.'

" 'Ah, we'll give you money enough to get home on,' they said. So we bet another six or seven hundred dollars.

"When we found a level spot we thought would do, we got out and stepped off 300 yards. The local folks and the rodeo crowd had heard there was a match brewing, so by the time we got the horses to the starting line, it looked like the whole town had migrated over.

"The crowd was pretty pro-Waggoner. Pretty soon, the bets were being laid down fast and furious. It seemed like all the money was on the Waggoner horse. In fact, there was only one man that I can recall that bet on Midnight.

"His name was Benny Binion, and he was from Dallas. Later on, he moved to Las Vegas and made a fortune in the gambling business.

"I had Midnight Jr. pretty well trained," Walter continues. "When we put the jockey saddle on him and scored him a few times, he knew there was a horse race coming.

"We rode up to the starting line with Midnight Jr. in a jockey saddle and Skip up on him. Mr. Waggoner said, 'Now son, you can't ride your horse in a flat saddle.

" 'Wasn't nothing said about the saddles,' I said. 'You ride your horse in whatever you want, and I'll do the same.

*Although he thought the price a fair one at the time, Walter has always maintained that selling Midnight Jr. was one of the biggest mistakes he ever made.*

"The race was lap-and-tap, which meant that the starter would let the horses go from a running start, as long as they were lapped a half-length on each other.

"Midnight Jr. knew what was coming, but that Waggoner Ranch horse didn't. I could see he hadn't been raced. The starting judge let them go the first time, and Midnight shot out of there so quick they called a mis-start. We brought 'em back and got 'em off again, and the same thing happened.

"I called Skip over and said, 'Skip, our horse is getting a little worked up. This time, let that bay gelding have about a length-and-a-half of daylight. We need to get this race underway.'

"Skip was a worrier, and half the money we'd bet was his. He said, 'I'll do it, but we might not get it back.' 'Oh yeah,' I said. 'We'll get it back on the second jump.'

"Skip had also found one more thing to be worried about. It was illegal to bet on horse races in Texas at the time, and E. Paul had gotten a couple of Texas Rangers to serve as finish line judges.'

" 'If this isn't a helluva note,' Skip said. 'Look down there at who we've got for finish line judges. Even if we win this damn thing, we ain't gonna be able to collect our winnings.' 'Oh yeah we will,' I said.

"On the third try, the race got started. The Waggoner gelding got off to about a three-length lead, because of the way I'd made Skip hold Midnight back. Midnight took the lead around three strides out, and it was all over from that point on. We outran the Waggoner horse by 30 feet or more.

"After the race, Mr. Waggoner came up to me and said, 'Young man, how's your little pony bred?' 'He's by Old Midnight,' I said. 'I should have known,' he replied. "No wonder we couldn't outrun him. I used to own his daddy.'

"And he did."

By Midnight Jr.'s 4-year-old year, by Walter's account, he had been match-raced 16 times. The black stallion's

record stood at 16 wins and 0 losses.

The future looked bright for Walter, Tien, and their Quarter Horse breeding and race program. Then, in the wink of an eye, everything changed.

"By the summer of 1941," Walter says, "Mr. H. S. Bissell of Las Cruces, New Mexico, got wind of Midnight Jr. He was the owner of the company that made the Bissell carpet sweepers. His ranch foreman, Charlie Combs, was from Cheyenne and that's how Mr. Bissell came to know about the horse.

"Anyway, he sent Charlie up that fall to try to buy Midnight. I didn't really want to sell him, but I priced him anyway. I told Charlie I'd take $1,000 for him. I thought that would scare him off.

"It didn't. They bought him on the spot.

"In September, I loaded Tien and Jimmie in the pickup, hopped Midnight Jr. up in the pickup and headed for Las Cruces.

"We got there, unloaded the horse and visited with the Bissell family for a while. We wound up staying overnight in Mr. Bissell's guest house and I don't think I got any sleep at all.

"Tien bawled all night because she didn't want me to sell the horse. Jimmie, who was 7 at the time, bawled because he didn't want me to sell him, either.

"The next morning, I went to Mr. Bissell and said, 'Mr. Bissell, I've gotten myself into a heck of a jam. My wife and son are upset with me for selling this horse. What would it cost for me to buy him back?'

" 'Walter, I can't sell him back to you,' he said. 'I need this horse for my breeding program. I will make you a promise, though. If I ever do decide to let him go, you'll be the first person I call.'

"I thanked him, and we all got in the truck and headed home. What else could I do? We'd shook hands on the deal. There was no way I could back out."

Upon his return to Oklahoma, Walter found himself with only half of

"Next to Midnight Jr., Revenue was my best early-day stallion."

a Quarter Horse breeding program.

The distaff side of it was alive and well. Even after acquiring his original six mares—the five A. D. Reed-bred ones and Joan—Walter had continued to seek out and add new mares.

By the fall of 1941, such well-bred animals as Sioux City Sue, a 1936 brown mare by Jeff Self by A. D. Reed, and out of Trixie by Ace by Peter McCue; Merrick's War Bonds, a 1936 brown mare by Cimarron by Jeff Self, and out of Salty; and Jean Marie, a 1940 chestnut mare by Silk McCue by Waggoner and out of Golden Wolf, were part of the Merrick broodmare band.

Most of the Merrick mares, and a few outside ones, were safe in foal to Midnight Jr. for 1942. Among the resulting foals, Bonnie Blue, a full sister to Grey Badger II; Chigger, the maternal grandsire of Sonny Dee Bar; and Butcher Boy, another Clint Higgins-bred stallion, stood out.

But Walter was still faced with the task of acquiring a replacement herd sire, and it took him several years to do so.

In the fall of 1943, he purchased Revenue, a good-looking yearling chestnut stallion by Young Midnight by Midnight, and out of Salty.

"Next to Midnight Jr.," Walter says, "Revenue was my best early-day stallion. He was a little bigger horse than 'Jr.', and had excellent conformation. I even showed him at halter a few times. I think he might have made a racehorse, too. But I rode him a little hard one day, working cattle, and he got his wind broke. But I used him as a sire for six seasons— from 1944 through 1949.

But even with Revenue in place as a sire, Walter regretted ever letting go of his first registered Quarter Horse.

"But I've often thought that selling Midnight Jr. was one of the biggest mistakes I ever made in the horse business," he says. "He was only a 4-year-old at the time, so he had his whole life ahead of him. I could already see he was going to make a good breeding horse.

"I guess I just didn't realize how good."

*To replace his foundation sire, Walter purchased Revenue P-2070, a Midnight Jr. three-quarter brother. A 1942 chestnut stallion by Young Midnight and out of Salty, Revenue was never raced but did go on to become a successful sire.*

# 7 SHADES OF GREY

*"I got a little nervous and tried to convince Walter not to make the match. He never seemed to worry much. He just looked at me and said, 'Aw, Skip . . . I believe we'll be all right. . . .' "*
—Skip Montgomery

*Grey Badger II remains one of the most legendary match-racers in the annals of Quarter Horse history. He is shown here, circa mid- to late 1940s, with young Wayne Cox in the irons.*

**Photo by Fort Worth Photo Lab,** *Courtesy* **The Quarter Horse** *Journal.*

*Bred by Walter Merrick, "Badger" was purchased as a yearling by Chick Crisp of Sayre, Oklahoma. Crisp, who owned the Sayre livestock yard, kept Badger penned there until the stallion was a 2-year-old.*
**Photos courtesy American Quarter Horse Heritage Center & Museum, Amarillo, Texas**

THE SALE of Midnight Jr. not only left Walter Merrick scrambling for a breeding replacement, it also put him temporarily out of the match racing business. In seeking a solution to the latter problem, the lanky cowboy had to look no further than his own breeding program.

"Grey Badger II was foaled on my ranch on May 5, 1941," Walter says. "With Midnight Jr. for a daddy and Grey Annie for a mama, he was bred to run. In fact, he traced to Billy the Tough twice and to Peter McCue four times.

"I almost didn't get the chance to race him, though. It seemed like I was always needing money in those days, so I sold him as a weanling for $500.

"Chick Crisp, the man who bought him, was a friend of mine from Sayre. He owned the Sayre livestock sale barn, and after he bought him, he put 'Badger' in one of the sale yard pens and just fed him and left him there. I don't believe the colt saw the outside of that pen until he was 2."

Even though he had sold Badger, Walter did not forget about the well-bred youngster. So, when the colt turned 2 and Walter was offered the chance to train and run him, he was quick to accept.

"Chick was known to take a drink now and then," Walter says. "One night in the spring of 1943, he'd been drinking and he called me up around 3 o'clock in the morning.

" 'Hey,' he said, 'I'm going to bring ol' Badger up there so you can break him. I've got him matched.'

" 'When's the race?' I asked.

" 'Thirty days from now,'

" 'Hell. I can't break that horse and have him ready in 30 days.'

" 'Oh yeah, you can. I'm bringing him up there.'

"So I got Badger out to the ranch and broke him to ride.

"My son Jimmie was 10 years old then, and he was the only light rider I had. I'd put him up on Badger and the horse would run about 50 yards and then buck the kid off. I guess he bucked him off four or five times. It got to where Jimmie wasn't wild about crawling back on. But he did, and we finally got the colt to where we could start conditioning him.

"Joan, my good Joe Hancock mare, was a year older than Badger," he continues. "We had been match racing her a little, and she had some speed. When I thought Badger was ready to be worked with another horse, I put Jimmie up on him and Tien up on Joan.

"I had a flat spot near the house where I could let my racehorses out a little. It didn't have a rail or anything, just a track that I'd worked up to make the ground a little softer.

"In those days, Tien was pretty gutsy. She'd try about anything, and she was really itchin' to ride a racehorse. I told her to be careful with Joan, though.

" 'After you take off,' I said, 'don't try to hold her in. Just let her go or she'll take the bit in her mouth and run off with you.'

"Well, the four of them took off, and sure enough, the first thing Tien did was get scared and try to haul the mare in. Joan took the bit in her mouth and lunged forward.

"The next thing I know, Tien—all 90 pounds of her—was up on the mare's neck. Then she was under the neck. And then she was on the ground and the mare ran over her.

"I ran up to where she was, and she was out cold. 'Now you've done it,' I said to myself. 'You've killed your wife.'

"But she came to and sat up. Outside of a few bumps and bruises, she was all right. And that was pretty much the last time she cared about riding a racehorse."

By hook or crook, Merrick and his family had Chick Crisp's gray colt ready to run within the allotted time.

"We ran Badger for the first time in May of 1943, at Sayre," Walter says. "We matched him for $1,000, lap-and-tap, against a mare owned by Mrs. Joe Van Vacter of Carter, Oklahoma. The mare's name was Black Bottom. She was a seasoned racehorse and Badger was as green as grass. Before we'd agree to the match, we got them to accept the clause that, if either horse bucked, the race was off.

"I had Skip up on Badger. The colt didn't buck, Skip stayed on, and we won the race."

Next up for the Merrick-trained 2-year-old was a 4th of July race that marked the first time Badger was required to break out of a starting gate.

"After Sayre, I took Grey Badger up to Woodward to a three-day race meet," Walter says. "Tien and Skip went with me, along with a couple of local boys who had gotten in the habit of following us around and betting on our horses. Dr. Bonafield, the dentist in Sayre, was one of them. He loved to bet on the horses and he wasn't bashful about laying his money down.

"The first night, we put Badger in a box stall and were just hanging around in front of it. A fella named Charlie Mitchell—he was from over near Fairfax—stopped by and said, 'What are you boys gonna' do with that gray colt?'

" 'We're going to match him, if we can,' I said.

" 'You can match him against the Thoroughbred mare in the next stall,' he said. 'I own her.'

" 'OK,' I said, 'We'll run you lap-and-tap.'

" 'No you won't,' he said. 'My mare's a gate horse, so if we run at all, it'll be out of a gate.'

"Well, Grey Badger had never been in a starting gate, so that evening, Skip and I took him to the track and broke him out of one. The next morning we did it again, this time with a seasoned gate horse alongside him. We figured that was about as much training as we were going to have time to get in."

Skip Montgomery—horse breeder, jockey and match-racing co-conspirator—recalls what transpired next.

"Walter was bound and determined to get in a horse race," he says. "I just wasn't sure he was gettin' in the right one.

"I got a little nervous and tried to convince Walter not to make the match. He never seemed to worry

## "You ain't gonna bet us no more money. We're poor boys and that colt is capable of bucking."

*Turned over to Walter to condition for racing, Grey Badger II was quickly whipped into racing shape. That's Tien at the halter of the speedy-looking colt.*

much. He just looked at me and said, 'Aw, Skip . . . I believe we'll be all right. . . .'

"So Walter matched that ol' boy for $1,500, and the race was at 275 yards.

"We were all relaxing up in the hotel room," he continues, "when that fella and some of his friends dropped by. One of them said, 'We'd like to bet you boys some more money.' 'You ain't gonna bet us no more money,' Walt said. 'We're poor boys and that colt is capable of bucking.'

"The mare's owner said, 'Well, you boys seem like good boys, but my mare is going to daylight your colt out of the gate.'

"I piped up at that point and said, 'I'll tell you what. All I got is this here hundred dollar bill, but I'll just bet it

*Originally a "lap-and-tap" brush track sprinter, Badger eventually graduated to more sophisticated venues. Here, he gets a good break from the gates at the Ada, Oklahoma, track in the mid-1940s.* **Photo by Orren Mixer, courtesy *The Quarter Horse Journal***

*Toward the end of his racing career, Grey Badger II made two starts at an American Quarter Racing Association-sanctioned meet held at the Fort Duncan racetrack. In the top photo, he defeats the highly regarded Nettie Hill in an October 27, 1945, 220-yard sprint. At the bottom, he wins his second start and qualifies for his AQRA "AA" Register of Merit.*

that your mare don't daylight the colt.' So we made the bet, they left, and I went to bed.

"The race was the next day. That mare's name was Queenie, as I recall. They loaded her in the gate, and we loaded Badger in next to her.

"I was sittin' up there, pretty as you please, and I happened to glance back over my shoulder at Walt. He had climbed up on the tailgate behind us and was taking off his belt.

" 'Damn it, Walt,' I said, 'Don't you hit this colt with that belt. He's liable to buck me off.'

" 'Well, Skip,' he said, 'I believe I'd take a'holt of him then, 'cause I'm gonna hit him.'

"Well, Walter spanked the colt on the rump and he shot out of there like a cannonball. The mare didn't daylight him out of the gate, either. In fact, he daylighted her and we won the race easy."

As much as they had tried to appear reluctant to bet any side money, Walter and his match-racing cronies had that as part of their game plan from the get go. Back in the hotel room on the evening after the contest, there was cause to celebrate.

"I imagine, between us all, we bet $7,000 or $8,000 on the race," Walter says. "I had made it a practice to have Tien do most of our side-betting.

"She was good at it. She'd go up into the grandstands and bet. She'd have bills wrapped around her fingers and be taking in bets from all sides.

"And I'd tell her, 'Now don't scatter your money. If you make a bet, you keep all the money until you see who wins.' She'd have her pockets full of money.

"Sometimes, after you'd won a match race, some of the side bets could get a little hard to find. When we'd match a bet with some ol' boy, we'd just say, 'If it's all right with you, we'll just let Tien hold the money.' She'd take their bet, match it with an equal amount of ours, and stash both bets away.

"She was just a little ol' slip of a thing, and those boys couldn't hardly

say that she looked like the type who was gonna run off with the money. And Tien loved that part of the deal.

"She only had one hard-and-fast rule when it came to betting. She always kept a two-dollar bill stashed away someplace; to make sure we'd have enough gas money to get home on.

"The night after the match race in Woodward," he continues, "we were all back in the hotel room. Tien was sitting up on the bed with her legs folded under her. She'd collected all our winnings and had it gathered in a big pile in front of her.

"It looked like there was a fortune there. Then she started divvying it up and we were all laughing and joking around.

"It felt good to be alive."

For the remainder of 1943 and all of 1944, Grey Badger II was left under Walter's care and training. The duo proved to be all but unbeatable. In the spring of 1944, however, they did suffer what would wind up being their only defeat as a team.

"Chick had matched a race in Seiling, Oklahoma, about 100 miles northeast of Sayre," Walter says. "The distance was 300 yards, and we were matched against a Thoroughbred mare named Pola Mandy. She was owned by J. E. Ogle of Waurika, Oklahoma. Pola Mandy had registered Thoroughbred papers, but she wasn't a purebred. She was sired by a horse named Polante (TB) and was out of Nona, by Joe Hancock. Later on, they registered her with the AQHA.

"The afternoon of the race, there came a big storm that blew the grandstand away and turned the track to slop. I could see there wasn't going to be any race, so I bedded Badger down in a box stall and fed him some grain and hay.

"Just as it was getting dark, here came Chick. 'Get the horse ready,' he said. 'We're gonna run us a race.'

" 'No we're not,' I said. 'I've put the horse up for the night.'

" 'Yes, we are,' he said. 'I've got it matched. If we don't run it, we'll forfeit the money.'

**Next up for Walter Merrick and Grey Badger II was the race that probably did more to establish both man and horse as match-racing legends than any other.**

" 'Well, all right,' I said. 'But I don't want nothing to do with the bet. I ain't gonna lose my money in the deal.'

"So I got Badger ready. The track was a half-mile oval. We couldn't run on the front side of the track because of all the debris from the grandstand. So we went to the backside and stepped off 300 yards.

"By this time, it was dark out. And I mean dark. You couldn't see your hand in front of your face. They lined up a bunch of cars against the outside railing, and had them turn their lights on. Skip Montgomery was up on Badger. We got the horses off, and they just kind of disappeared into the night.

"I went sloshing down the track after them. I went a ways, then stopped and asked the crowd who was ahead at that point. 'The gray horse was,' they all said. I walked a little farther, asked the same question and got the same answer. When I got to the finish line I asked, 'Who won it?' 'The sorrel mare did,' they said.

"Pretty soon, here come Skip and Badger, back up the track. 'What happened?,' I asked.

" 'I'll tell you what happened,' he said. 'There was no way in hell I was gonna take this SOB full-speed around the turn in the dark. I pulled him up. Go see if you can re-match it.'

"So I went back and tried to get those boys to run again. They just laughed at me."

By mid-year, Walter had decided that he would make a bid to re-purchase Grey Badger. In partnership with Clarence Hadlock, the local druggist, he offered $8,000 for the now-seasoned sprinter. Chick Crisp accepted it.

Next up for Walter Merrick and Grey Badger II was the race that probably did more to establish both man and horse as match-racing legends than any other. This was, of course, "the race that broke the bank."

The race took place in September of 1944 at Cheyenne, Oklahoma. A group of horsemen from Pampa, Texas—located about 60 miles to the west—had a fast runner from South Texas that they felt could take the measure of Grey Badger. Named Pee Wee, the horse was reputed to be a son of Joe Moore—Ott Adams' famous speed sire.

The Texans arrived in Cheyenne brimming with confidence and eager to place some side bets. So eager was one livestock buyer from the Lone

*After his racing days were over, Badger went on to become a renowned sire. Badgerette, a 1944 gray mare out of Roan Lady by Joe Reed P-3, was one of his first sale-topping get.*

Star State, that he bet $800 that Pee Wee would daylight Badger at 10 paces.

The Cheyenne country crowd, having spent several years lining their pockets with proceeds gained from backing Merrick racers, was just as ready to accommodate their neighbors from the west.

When the only bank in Cheyenne opened on the morning of the race, it was reported to have had $56,000 in its vaults. By noon, its patrons had withdrawn so much money that the bank had to send out to the neighboring communities of Elk City and Sayre for enough cash to do business. Every store in Cheyenne was likewise reported to have exchanged all their cash for checks written by the locals to cover their bets.

By the time the two horses approached the starting line that afternoon, the Cheyenne Bank had been forced to temporarily shut its doors. The race was a 300-yard contest, and Grey Badger II, with Skip Montgomery in the irons, emerged victorious.

The Texans returned home, somewhat disheartened and considerably poorer, while the Cheyenne bank re-opened the next day with its coffers overflowing.

In the summer of 1945, Walter once again relinquished ownership of Grey Badger. This time, he sold him to a man who would become a lifelong friend and supporter—Oscar Cox of Lawton, Oklahoma.

"I had gotten well-acquainted with Oscar through the racing," Walter says. "He was a match race man and he had some excellent horses. He had a Louisiana connection and brought some tough runners into this country from there. He had some top race mares during the early to mid-1940s, and later owned Blob Jr. and Josie's Bar when they were both World Champion Quarter Running Horses.

"Oscar had a big car dealership in Lawton. He was a heavy-set man who loved to race horses, gamble and have fun. We got to where we were pretty good friends and he and another

Lawton man named Willie Shrum bought Badger from me in the summer of 1945 for $8,000."

For a short while after acquiring Grey Badger, Cox left the stallion in Walter's care and training. That fall, they ran two big races in Amarillo, Texas.

"The first race we matched," Walter says, "was against a mare named Nancy Hance. She was a daughter of My Texas Dandy and was owned by Lewis Blackwell of Amarillo. Lewis had built a match-racing track just south of town, and that's where we ran. We matched it for $5,000 at a distance of 300 yards.

"After we won that race," he continues. "an old racehorse trainer by the name of Blaine Speers got on the track loudspeaker. He was training a mare named Squaw H.—a daughter of King—for J. O. Hankins of Rocksprings, Texas.

"She was a tough runner and Mr. Speers announced he would match a 300-yard race against either Grey Badger or Nancy Hance the following week for $10,000.

"Oscar was busy collecting his money and he didn't hear the announcement. So I went running over to him and told him what was up. He went straight over to Mr. Speers and made the match, and the next weekend we hauled Badger back to Amarillo.

"He wound up beating Squaw H. too, and for a while I was afraid we weren't going to make it out of Texas in one piece. I guess Squaw H. was quite a favorite with those Amarillo boys."

And still the challengers kept showing up. One, a prosperous wheat farmer from Kansas, paid an especially steep price to find out Merrick's runner was not to be taken lightly.

"In the late fall of 1945," Walter says, "John Platt from Hardtner, Kansas, brought a top gelding named Big Foot Charley—a Burnett Ranch-bred son of old Joe Hancock—to run against Badger in a 300-yard race. Oscar matched him for $1,000 for the

"I didn't care what anyone thought of him. I knew he was a runner. And the years I spent matching him were among the most enjoyable of my entire life."

*In November of 1949, Grey Badger II and his son Grey Badger III were acquired by the Burnett Ranch. The two stallions went on to found a great dynasty of show and ranch horses. Long-time Burnett Ranch manager Rex Keith is seen at Grey Badger II's halter in this shot taken in the mid-1950s.*

**Photo by Franklin Reynolds, courtesy of *The Quarter Horse Journal***

first 220 yards, and another $1,000 for the whole 300 yards.

"After we outran his horse to both points, we gathered in Mr. Platt's car to collect our winnings. He reached in his glove box and took out a rolled up newspaper. He unrolled it, took out a big wad of bills, and started paying off his debts.

"After he was finished, he held up a single bill. 'Lookie here, boys,' he said. 'I come down here with $20,000 in this newspaper. This $100 bill is all I've got left.' "

In the fall of 1945, Cox took Grey Badger home with him to Lawton. He ran him several more times that year, at an AQRA-sanctioned race held at Fort Duncan Race Track in Eagle Pass, Texas. There, the now 4-year-old stallion won both of his starts, set a track record for 220 yards, and achieved his Register of Merit in racing.

Four years later, Cox decided to scale back his horse operation. After arriving at the decision, the first

person he contacted was his friend Walter Merrick.

"I suppose it was sometime in September or October of 1949 that Oscar called me," Walter says. "He said, 'Walter, I'm cutting way back in the horse business. I've got 40 head or so that I'm needin' to sell, and I want you to get down here and load 'em all up.

" 'Oscar, I can't afford to buy that many horses,' I said.

" 'You just get down here,' he said. 'I'll make it to where you can afford it.'

"And he did.

"I got some great horses in that deal," Walter continues. "Grey Badger was in the package. So were a couple of great match-race mares named Miss Ruby, Beggar Girl and Tom's Lady Grey. There was also some nice young Grey Badger horses, including a gray 3-year-old filly named Tidy M.

"Hank Wilson, a good friend of mine from Arnett, had bred Tidy M. I'd trained her for racing and we won a trial heat of the first Oklahoma

Quarter Horse Exhibitor's Association in Enid. The filly had the fastest time in the trials, but we had bad luck in the finals with her."

There was also one other especially noteworthy horse that Walter Merrick acquired from Oscar Cox in the package. This was Grey Badger III, a 2-year-old gray colt out of an ex-race mare named Mary Greenock (TB).

In November of 1949, Walter sold both Grey Badgers to the Burnett Ranch.

Grey Badger II, of course, went on to become a noted sire of race, ranch and show horses. He passed away on the ranch in 1972, at the age of 31.

Grey Badger III was likewise a top sire, particularly when it came to broodmares.

One of his daughters, Sugar Badger, became the dam of Peppy San Badger, National Cutting Horse Association (NCHA) Futurity and Derby winner, and cutting horse legend. Another daughter, Triangle Tookie, produced five AQHA Champions, including Two Eyed Jack, the all-time leading sire of AQHA Champions.

"I guess Grey Badger II was the greatest match-racing horse I ever had anything to do with," Walter says. "Usually, after you win three or four match races with a horse, people quit running at you.

"But they didn't with Badger. They'd just keep trying. They'd say, 'We ought to be able to beat that horse.'

"He didn't look like a racehorse. In fact, one ol' boy who didn't like either me or Badger used to call him a '4th of July horse.' I don't know what he meant by that . . . probably that Badger was some kind of backyard horse who'd only show up at the races once a year.

"I didn't care what anyone thought of him. I knew he was a runner. And the years I spent matching him and his daddy were among the most enjoyable of my entire life.

"They were the years that Tien and I first started realizing that life could get a little better; the years that we first started daring to try to make get that way.

"They were the best of times, and I wouldn't mind living every single moment of them all over again."

*Even in his mid-teens, Badger still demonstrates the balance and powerful muscling of a sprinting champion.*
**Photo courtesy of**
***The Quarter Horse Journal***

# 8 KIDS, CALVES AND COLTS

*"It was a good ranch; as good as a little ranch can be. I knew I was gonna make a bid on it by the time we got back to the house."*
—Walter Merrick

JUST AS his match-racing days with Midnight Jr. and Grey Badger II had convinced Walter Merrick it was possible to breed and race better horses, so did his days as a Davis Ranch cowboy convince him that it was possible to own a bigger and better ranch.

His purchase of the Salt Grass Section in the late 1930s had started him out in the right direction as a landowner. By the time 1942 rolled around, however, things there were beginning to get a little cramped.

To begin with, his Quarter Horse- and Hereford cattle-breeding programs had both increased in size to the point where his 640 acres of

*Walter Merrick's Crawford, Oklahoma, ranch, shown here in 1960 was purchased for cash in the fall of 1945. Walter's share of the proceeds from the first Quarter Horse production sale ever held in the Sooner State financed the transaction.*

*During the late 1940s and 1950s, Walter purchased several large groups of mares to increase the size of his broodmare band and augment his horse sale offerings. Included among them were this band of "Heart-branded" mares from the L. C. Moorhouse Ranch of Santa Rosa, New Mexico.*

land was overstocked.

The dugout—all two rooms of it—was now home to Walter, Tien, Jimmie, Donna and Fannie Lou Merrick. It, too, was full to the point of bursting.

Then, in June of 1942, Champ Davis passed away at the age of 84. Shortly thereafter, his part of the ranch was sold to R. D. Mills of Pampa, Texas. In Walter's mind, the time to move on had arrived.

"Champ Davis was like a second father to me," Walter says. "He was always looking out for me and my family, and when he passed away I knew things at the ranch would never be the same.

"So I sold the Salt Grass Section and leased a 2,000-acre ranch seven miles west of Cheyenne. I moved my family onto it, and then went back and drove my stock over. At that time, I had 150 head of cattle and 12 to 15 head of horses.

"In the spring of 1943, that ranch got sold to the government and I had to vacate it. So I found work managing a 50-section spread 25 miles north of Cheyenne, near the little town of Arnett. We lived in a four-room farmhouse 12 miles south of Arnett, and Jim Bradshaw, the owner of that ranch, leased me six sections to run my livestock on."

Shortly after taking up residence on the Bradshaw Ranch, Walter received some sobering news in the mail.

"In 1944, World War II was in full swing in Europe," he says. "That same year, I received my notice to report for active duty. I knew I had to go, so I started putting my affairs in order.

"Shortly after I'd gotten the notice, the county extension agent drove out to the ranch from Cheyenne. He pulled up, got out of his car and walked over to where I was working. 'Walter,' he said, 'I hear you've been called up.' 'You heard right,' I told him. 'Do you want to go?' he asked. 'I don't reckon anyone wants to go,' I said. 'But I don't see as how I've got any choice in the matter. They've told me to report, and that's what I intend to do.'

" 'I know that,' he said. 'But we need men like you here at home. You're doing the work of three men here on this ranch, so I'm going to put in for an agricultural exemption for you.' And that's what he did. It was approved and I never had to go to war."

As previously detailed, it was while working on the Bradshaw Ranch that Walter trained and raced Grey Badger II. It was also during this timeframe that he bred what was to become arguably the greatest daughter of Midnight Jr.

"In 1943," he says, "I took Joan down to Mr. Bissell's to breed to Midnight Jr. The following spring, she foaled a beautiful black filly.

"When she was a yearling, the filly came down with distemper and

*Hot Heels, a 1944 black mare by Midnight Jr. and out of Joan, was one of the ranch's first great matrons. An early bout with distemper kept the speedy-looking mare from the track, but she went on to become the dam of such AAA-rated runners as Mona Leta, Bob's Folly, Bar Heels, Johnny Do It and Mary Sunshine.*

**Photo courtesy American Quarter Horse Heritage Center & Museum, Amarillo, Texas**

abscessed on all four ankles. We treated her with sulpha and she healed up OK, but she had white scars from where she'd broke open. So we registered her as Hot Heels.

"By the time she was 2," he continues, "she was sound enough to break to ride. And she was fast. Jimmie rode her in a pony race once in Cheyenne. There must have been 30 or 40 ponies in that race.

"Before the race, I said to him, 'Just make sure you're not caught in the middle of that pack of ponies at the start. Take her to the outside and you'll be all right.' He did like I told him and Hot Heels just ran off and hid from the rest of the field."

Blemishes notwithstanding, Hot Heels went on to become one of the premier race producers in the breed.

It was also while he was living at Arnett that Walter added a third specialty to his horse-related money-making bag of tricks. He became involved in Quarter Horse production sales.

"In the summer of 1945," he says, "Leonard Milligan, who lived up near Nash, Oklahoma, paid me a visit. Leonard was a rodeo man—a calf roper and bulldogger. But he was

breeding horses, too. He knew I had good horses, so he suggested that we put on a horse sale together. That sounded like a good idea to me, so I agreed.

"Revenue was doing me a pretty good job as a sire. And I'd been picking up a good mare here and there and making my annual trip to the Burnett Ranch to pick over their yearling fillies. So, all told, I guess I was up to around 25 or 30 head.

"We held the sale in the fall of 1945 at Leonard's ranch. He had a big hay barn, and we cleaned it out and set up a ring and some bleachers. We didn't have a sale catalog. We just printed up a handbill listing the horses and their breeding. As far as I can tell, it was the first breeders' production sale ever held in the state of Oklahoma.

"I sold 20 or 22 head there, including Joan. She topped the sale and was purchased by Frank Hoffman, the well-known artist from Taos, New Mexico. Leonard had consigned some nice horses to the sale, too, so we both got along real well."

In late fall of 1945, with his horse sale windfall safely in hand, Walter's thoughts turned once again to ranching. After spending three years either on leased ground or working for someone else, he decided it was once again time to look for a permanent home.

"While I was working on the Bradshaw Ranch," he says, "I became aware of a ranch that was for sale over by Crawford. I got in touch with the man who owned it, and he told me to come over and he'd show it to me. So, one Sunday morning, I did.

"It was a 2,000-acre ranch. It wasn't a big ranch, but it set real pretty, right on the banks of the Canadian River. The house and barns set down in a hollow, sheltered on all sides by either hills or trees. It was a good ranch; as good as a little ranch could be.

"Right after I arrived, we saddled up a couple of horses and rode all over the ranch. We came back to the house and he said, 'Let's go in and get a cup of coffee.' I knew I was gonna make a bid on it when we got back to the house, but I thought I ought to try to get the price down a little bit.

"He priced it to me for $25,000. I said, 'I like your ranch and I'm going to try to buy it, but I think your price is a little high. If you'll take $500 off it, I'll take it and pay you cash money.'

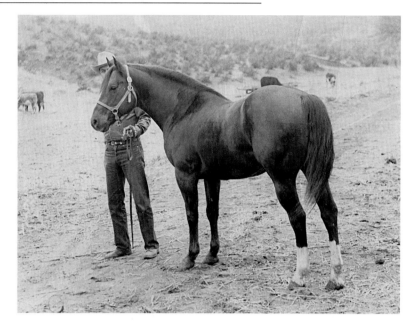

'I'll take $500 off if you'll let me keep half the mineral rights,' he said. Minerals didn't mean anything to me. I didn't think they were worth anything. So I just traded with him.

"Those minerals got to be high."

Compared to the houses the Merricks had lived in during the previous 15 years of their marriage, the Crawford Ranch homestead was a castle.

*Revenue, shown here with Walter at the halter, served as the Merrick Ranch's main herd sire for seven years—from 1943 through 1950.*

*Revenue H., a Merrick-bred son of Revenue, went on to become a race Register of Merit qualifier and a top calf roping horse and sire.*
**Photo by Ralph Morgan, courtesy *The Quarter Horse Journal***

*The Merrick broodmares (above and below) roamed at will over the Crawford Ranch's 2,000 scenic acres. That's Walter on the dun gelding in the background of the top shot.*

At first, it was just four rooms. In time, however, Walter added to both sides of it. On the east side he built two bedrooms and a bathroom. On the west side, he built a utility room, half-bath and office. After three years, electricity and indoor plumbing were also added, marking the first time in their lives that the family lived in a home with either.

An apartment for a hired hand was added to the top of an existing two-car garage, and a big, L-shaped concrete block building—housing a four-stall mare motel, two-stall stud barn and a breeding shed—was built onto the north and west sides of the existing barn. An extensive set of

corrals and horse runs rounded out the livestock complex.

All in all, the Crawford Ranch represented the first permanent home the Merricks felt they had ever lived in. So comfortable were they there that they even put in a conversation piece.

"A friend of mine owned a graveyard monument place in Sayre," Walter says. "He decided he was going to build me a fireplace, for free. He made it all out of marble, and carved the '14' brand into it. It was big and heavy, and it seemed like it took everybody in the country to put it up. But he had it polished off real good and it was a beautiful thing."

Bolstered by their success the

previous year, Walter and Leonard put on their second horse sale in Nash, Oklahoma, in the fall of 1946. As happened in the first sale, some of the Merrick offerings topped the second event.

"I put a pair of really nice yearling fillies, named Badgerette and Goldie, in the second sale," Walter says. "Badgerette was a gray, sired by Grey Badger II and out of Roan Alice by Joe Reed P-3. Goldie was a sorrel, sired by Revenue and out of Jodie by Joe Hancock.

"I got $1,600 for Badgerette and $1,500 for Goldie. Frank Wood of Sumner, Nebraska, bought them both. He went on to become a well-known Quarter Horse breeder in Nebraska, and those two fillies were the first registered horses he'd ever bought."

After the second Merrick-Milligan sale, it would be several years before Walter participated in another one. In the ensuing five years, life for he and his family settled into a comfortable rhythm. The two Merrick children were enrolled in the local school. Sherry Lynn "Lynnie" Merrick, the couple's third child, was born on February 24, 1948.

The years began to revolve around the seasons: spring, calving and foaling; summer, putting up feed; fall, shipping cattle; winter, forting up and feeding.

Walter continued to expand his Quarter Horse breeding and racing program. In addition to utilizing Revenue as a sire, he began taking mares out to breed to such horses as Grey Badger II and Los Molinos (TB), both of whom stood in Lawton at Oscar Cox's facility; Piggin String (TB), who stood in Tucson, Arizona; and Leo, who stood in Perry, Oklahoma, at Bud Warren's place.

In the fall of 1950, Merrick also acquired a second stud. This was Monterrey, a 1940 palomino sired by Pretty Boy and out of a mare by Waggoner's Rainy Day P-13.

"Monterrey was a real good-looking horse who had been bred by the Waggoner Ranch," Walter says. "He'd gotten crippled as a colt, so the

Waggoners had sold him to Ellis Locke and Orval Christopher of Miami, Texas—over near Pampa. I bought him from them.

"I guess most people would consider Monterrey more of a ranch horse than a racehorse," he continues. "But he traced to Harmon Baker and Peter McCue on the top, and Rainy Day by Midnight on the bottom. So he had a little speed behind him. And he passed it on, too. He sired such AAA-rated runners as Mission Boy and Wilson's Yellow Cat, and they were out of ranch-bred mares."

In addition to the new stallions and mares that Walter had added to his breeding program in the late 1940s and early 1950s, he was even able to re-acquire a pair of foundation horses that he had sold earlier. And the first one to re-appear just happened to be the very horse he'd started his program with.

"One day in the fall of 1949," he says, "Mr. Bissell's daughter and son-in-law, Dorothy and Ed Cox, showed up at the ranch. 'We were sent up here to see if you wanted old Jr. back,' Ed said.

"Well, I'd heard that Mr. Bissell had turned down $20,000 for the horse

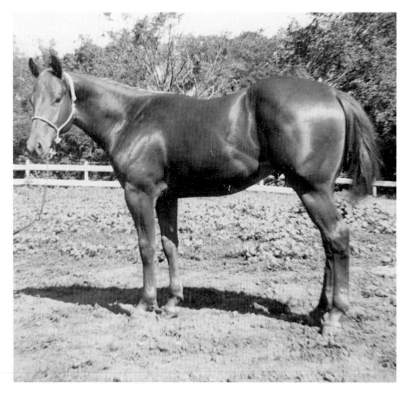

*Little Lady Wood, a 1945 sorrel filly by Revenue and out of Jodie by Joe Hancock, was one of the sale toppers at the 1946 Merrick-Milligan production sale. She was purchased for $1,500 by Frank Wood of Sumner, Nebraska.*

from some people in Old Mexico. So I said, 'You know I'd like him back, but I haven't got the kind of money it'd take to buy him.'

" 'He ain't gonna cost you anything but a trip to New Mexico to pick him up,' he said. 'The old man has decided to give him to you.'

"Man, I got right in my truck and went and got him.

"In March of 1950," he continues, "I went to breed the first mares to Midnight. I turned him into a corral next to some mares. He ran over to them and danced around a little bit, then he dropped to the ground and died. I always reckoned he had a heart attack, but after studying on it, I've come to see it different.

"Right before he ran over to those mares, Midnight stopped and grabbed a mouthful of oats from a grain box I'd set up for him. Then he let out one of those stud nickers—the kind where the horse would suck air in as he made the sound.

"The way I figure it now, he got some oats down his windpipe and choked to death. If I'd thought of it back then, I'd have got my jackknife out and opened him up so he could get some air.

*Sport, a 1947 chestnut gelding by Grey Badger II and out of Slipper B. by Tom B., serves as a good example of the type of dual-purpose race and ranch horses that Walter Merrick was breeding during the early Crawford years. Hired hand Pat Thompson, who went on to become a noted Quarter Horse breeder and racehorse trainer in his own right, is in the saddle.*

"I've often wondered how it would have played out if I'd gotten the use of him for another five or seven years. He was only 13 years old when he died, and I had better mares to breed him to. In a few years, I could have even crossed him on some Three Bars (TB) mares.

"But I lost him before I could even get a mare bred to him."

Oddly enough, the second foundation horse to find her way back into the Merrick program wound up not staying in place very long, either.

"In the fall of 1951," he said, "Tien and I were at the races in Albuquerque, New Mexico. I was in the race office one day and happened to pick up a sale catalog. They were having the sale the next day, and I saw that Joan, my old original Burnett Ranch mare, was consigned to it. I said to Tien, 'We're not going to the races tomorrow. We're going to this sale and I'm going to try and buy Joan back.'

"I had sold her in my first sale for $1,500. At the time she went through the New Mexico sale, she had a nice filly at her side by a Thoroughbred horse named Chickamauga and she was back in foal to him. I was able to get her bought back for $1,200.

"In 1952," he continues, "Joan had a bay colt that I named Taos Joe. I raised another good colt from her the next year, and then she died."

As the decade of the 1950s dawned, the winds of change were blowing in the world of Quarter Horse racing.

Back roads, brush tracks and lap-and-tap Sunday starts were giving way to graded surfaces, starting gates and organized race meets. The heyday of the neighborhood match racehorse was over. The days of pari-mutuel racing had begun.

While he lamented the end of the daring and "living large" era of match racing, Walter Merrick welcomed the advent of better-organized and more uniformly graded competition.

And, as he had throughout all of his life, the Oklahoma horseman was quick to adjust his thinking to accommodate the new climate.

As evidenced by this 1956 winter shot of Walter and 8-year-old Lynnie preparing to throw some "cake" out to the cattle, life was not all fun and games on the Crawford Ranch. According to Walter, that's a "good Revenue gelding" Lynnie's mounted on.

Joe Merrick, the youngest member of the Merrick clan, grew up on the Crawford Ranch. He is pictured here at age 3, mounted on the good ranch and pony gelding Lucky 14.

# PART 2

# A MAN FOR ALL AGES

# 9 CHANGING LANES

*"We were getting her ready for the race when a guy stopped by and asked, 'What's that 14 on her hip stand for?' 'That's gonna be her time,' I said."*
—*Walter Merrick*

*Jean Marie, a 1940 chestnut mare by Peter Roan and out of Golden Wolf, was one of the Walter Merrick-trained racehorses that bridged the gap between the brush track and pari-mutuel eras. She is shown below in 1950, winning a race in Ada, Oklahoma.*

THERE WERE several compelling reasons behind the sudden demise of Quarter Horse match racing in the mid- to late 1940s. The first had to do with increased mobility and improved communication.

World War II had come to an end, and so had the days of automobile, gasoline and tire rationing. America was back on the move and more mobile than ever.

And then there was the telephone. All of a sudden, phones had become commonplace in the outlying rural areas of the West. Party lines were the order of the day, and it became a simple matter of picking up the phone to catch up on all the latest news and gossip—whether you were supposed to be on the line or not.

As a result, it became harder for Walter Merrick and other match-racing horsemen to travel anywhere regionally where the locals had not already heard of them and their racing exploits. Matches became increasingly hard to make.

The second contributing factor in the demise of match racing was the advent and rapid spread of organized Quarter Horse racing.

On February 1, 1945, the American Quarter Racing Association (AQRA) was founded in Tucson, Arizona, by Jim Haskell and a small group of "short horse" aficionados. Not a

blood registry, the association's main purpose was to identify horses for racing and devise a uniform method by which their performance could be graded.

The AQRA rating system took into account such things as prior performance, track conditions and assigned weights to grade racehorses as "D," "C," "B," "A," and "AA" performers. If a horse ran a race in "A" and "AA" time, he or she qualified for an AQRA Register of Merit award. (By January of 1952, the times had improved to the point that a "AAA" rating had to be added.)

By the late 1940s, the AQRA was sanctioning meets at locations in Arizona, New Mexico, Texas, Colorado and California. In 1949, recognizing the growing popularity of organized racing and the need for a unified effort to maintain it, Haskell put an initiative in motion that resulted in the AQRA being absorbed by the AQHA. As a result, the latter organization's racing division was born. Van Smelker Jr., one of Haskell's

assistants, was named its first head.

Back in Crawford, Oklahoma, Walter Merrick was doing a little restructuring of his own.

"There was a period of around five years," he says, "lasting from 1945 to 1950, where I wasn't too active in racing. I continued to match race some, but, mainly I just concentrated on ranching. During that time, I built my cow and calf operation up to around 300 pairs.

"After the two sales I had with Leonard Milligan in 1945 and 1946, my horse numbers were down, so I had to concentrate on building them back up. And I was more than willing to do that. As far as the horses went, the AQHA had turned them into a valuable commodity. Any kind of decent Quarter Horse that had papers was worth some money."

AQHA records reveal that in 1945, Walter registered 12 foals. The following year, he registered only three. All 15 were sired by either Grey Badger II or Revenue.

The year 1948 was even slower.

*Sheelgo, a 1945 bay mare by Stormy Don and out of Dusty Day, was the first Merrick-trained runner to achieve a AAA race rating. She is shown here in March 1949, after winning a 330-yard sprint at the Tucson, Arizona, race meet. Walter stands at the well-built mare's head while renowned female jockey Wantha Davis is in the irons.*

Only two Merrick-bred foals were registered with the association that year. One was sired by Revenue, and the other by Leo. By 1949 and 1950, the ranch's broodmare band had been increased in size to the point that eight foals were registered. Their sires were Grey Badger II, Revenue, Piggin String (TB) and Ranger Hancock.

By the time the new decade rolled around, Walter was ready to once again hit the horse racing road. This time, he picked as his target a pari-mutuel track.

"In the summer of 1949," he says, "I decided to take a string of racehorses up to run at a pari-mutuel meet in Kremmling, Colorado. I hired a man to stay at the ranch and look after things, and I loaded up around six horses and headed north.

"I had a Chevrolet truck with stock racks on the back of it that I hauled the horses in. Kenneth Brittian, my jockey, rode with me, and Tien and the kids followed in the car.

"Probably the fastest horse I took

with me on the trip was a mare named Sheelgo. She was a 1945 bay mare, sired by Stormy Don by Midnight Jr., and out of Dusty Day, a Waggoner Ranch mare. Sheelgo was owned by Hank Wilson, a neighbor and friend of mine from over around Arnette, and she was a AA-rated runner back when that was the highest rating. Later on, when they came up with a AAA rating, she qualified for that too.

"Another horse I took was Ranger Hancock. He was a 1943 roan stallion by Roan Hancock and out of a Burnett mare by Red Buck. 'Ranger' was owned by Gober Lee Mitchell of Canadian, Texas, and he had been a good match-racing horse in our part of the country for several years. He wasn't quite as fast as Sheelgo, but he'd really try for you and he did earn his AA rating.

"Hank Wilson also had a half-brother to Sheelgo that we took. His name was Lindy W., and he was a 1947 sorrel gelding by Little Mike and

*Lindy W., an early-day Merrick-trained ROM racehorse, was campaigned in the early 1950s at pari-mutuel tracks in Arizona, Colorado and Wyoming.*

out of Dusty Day. I won a few races with him, but he wasn't really a racehorse. He never did qualify for his Register of Merit."

The Kremmling race meet of 1949 was a three-week affair, with the horses only running on Fridays, Saturdays and Sundays. It was the track management's first experience with pari-mutuel, and, to say the least, everyone connected with the event was excited about it.

"For me and my family," Walter says, "the trip to Colorado was like a vacation. We stayed in a motel and did a little sightseeing on non-racing days.

"I think the folks who put on the meet were having just as much fun. They'd never run under pari-mutuel before. They didn't even have regular betting windows or a tote board. They hauled in a machine from somewhere to take care of all that.

"A friend of mine named John Hanson, from North Platte, Nebraska, came up one weekend to watch the races. I had Ranger in a race and he put a bet down on him.

"The horse won the race, and John figured he had around $350 coming. The pari-mutuel clerk got excited and paid him $3,500 instead.

"He tried to tell her she'd overpaid him, but she got flustered and said, 'You just take the money and get out of my way. I've got other people waiting.'

"So he put the money in his pocket and walked down to the barn where I was cooling the horse down. 'Lookie here, Walter,' he said. 'We got money now!' "

After the Kremmling meet was over, the Merrick caravan headed north and east, to a place and an event that Walter had been hankering to participate in since his days on the open range.

"I had always wanted to attend the Cheyenne Frontier Days," he said. "So, after the Colorado meet was over, we loaded up and headed for Wyoming.

"The meet there wasn't as long as the Kremmling one, and it wasn't

pari-mutuel. But we had another great time. All our horses won some races, and we got to take in the rodeo and the Frontier Days celebration, too. After it was over, we headed back home."

For the remainder of 1949, Walter concentrated on ranching. Then, in the spring of the following year, the race bug bit him once again.

"In March of 1950," he says, "I put together a string of four or five horses to take to a race meet in Tucson, Arizona. I still had Hank's two horses, Sheelgo and Lindy W., in training. In fact, on this trip, Hank came with me.

"I also took a horse by the name of Nellie Bly Pendhall. She was a 1945 bay mare by Joe Reed P-3, out of a Thoroughbred mare named Neat. She was owned by Art Pendhall of Clinton, Oklahoma. She wasn't as fast as Sheelgo, but she did win a race or two and qualified for her Register of Merit.

"Back then, there were two Quarter Horse racetracks in Tucson. One was the Rillito track and the other was the Rodeo track. It was on the fairgrounds, and we raced there.

"The Tucson meet lasted around 30 days, and Hank and I stayed at one of the local motels and took our meals at a nearby restaurant. We had a good meet, and it felt good to know my horses could be competitive that far from home."

After the meet was over, Walter returned to his ranch to prepare for his third Quarter Horse sale.

"While we were in Tucson," he says, "Hank Wilson and I decided to have a joint production sale. It was held on April 12, 1950, at Cheyenne.

"I had bought that big package of horses from Oscar Cox the fall before. I cut back the top end of the mares and young horses from it, to keep, and put the rest in the sale.

"I had a young Colorado cowboy named Pat Thompson working for me by this time. Pat was a good hand and he started a lot of the young horses that I consigned to the sale. He was with me for a couple of years, and

"After the sale, I started thinking about racing again."

*Mona Leta, a 1949 bay mare by Leo and out of Hot Heels, was the first Merrick-bred horse to become a world champion runner. She is shown here after winning a yearling race at Lawton, Oklahoma, on December 24, 1950.*

*In the finals of the 1951 Oklahoma Futurity at Enid, Mona Leta finished so far ahead of her rivals that track stewards initially lost sight of her and awarded the race to the second-place finisher. At the vocal insistence of the crowd, they reviewed the win photo and corrected their mistake.*

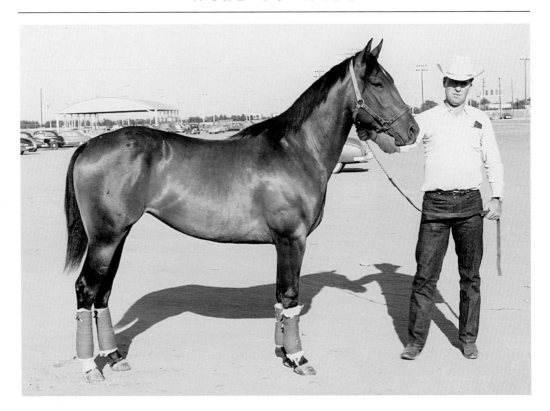

*On the day after the Oklahoma Futurity, Mona Leta was shown by Ed Cox of Las Cruces, New Mexico, at halter. The speedy-looking filly failed to place.*

then he went into racehorse breeding and training on his own around Sterling, Colorado.

"He trained a lot of good horses for Jack Casement up there, horses like Alfaretta, Old Tom Cat, She Kitty and Little Chloe. He also had a pair of top studs named Wiggy Bars and Jet Threat. But he got his start with me.

"Among the Oscar Cox horses that I sold in the 1950 sale," he continues, "were such good old race mares as Lucky Sloan, Miss Paducah, Mary Greenock (TB) and Tom's Lady Gray, and such old foundation mares as Sioux City Sue and Merrick's War Bonds.

"I also put Revenue in the sale, and he topped it. A man named Pete Becker from Ogallala, Nebraska, bought him for $1,025. Pete is still in the Quarter Horse business, and we've stayed in touch over the years. Revenue was his first top stud, and I've heard that he is credited with doing a lot to get the Quarter Horse breed established in Nebraska.

"To round out the sale, I consigned a nice set of Grey Badger II yearlings, 2-year-olds and 3-year-olds.

"After the sale, I started thinking about racing again."

In 1948, Walter had taken Hot Heels to the court of Bud Warren's great race sire, Leo. The result was a bay 1949 filly named Mona Leta. Although the lanky Oklahoma racehorse trainer, now in his late 30s, had achieved near-legendary status as a match racer, and had also proven that his charges could run and win on distant tracks, Walter was still only a regional celebrity.

Mona Leta changed all of that. More than any other of his racehorses had, the diminutive bay Midnight Jr. granddaughter spread Walter's fame as a racehorse man throughout the land.

"When Mona Leta was still a baby," he says, "a bunch of us local boys had gotten together and decided to match a yearling race. There were 10 of us, and we each put up $100. The race was a winner-take-all. The distance was set at 250 yards and the race was run on Christmas Eve day, at Enid.

"Because she was still a yearling, I didn't really train Mona Leta too hard. All I did was get her broke enough not to buck anybody off and breeze her a little.

"We took her up to Enid and were getting her ready for the race when a

*Here's a great sequence of shots of Mona Leta winning her trial heat of the 1951 Rocky Mountain Quarter Horse Futurity over Robin Reed and Leolita. In the winner's circle shot, Donna and Tien Merrick are to the left, with Oscar Cox behind them. Walter is next, then an unidentified handler. Jockey Edward Garza is up on Mona Leta, holding 3-year-old Lynnie Merrick.*

**Photo by Ralph Morgan**

guy stopped by and asked, 'What's that 14 on her hip stand for?' 'That's gonna be her time,' I said.

"And it was. She ran that race in 14 seconds flat and won it."

Mona Leta's next start, and her first official one, would not take place for more than seven months. On August 5, 1951, at Meade, Kansas, she won a 300-yard race in :16.4 under a strong hold.

From there, it was back to Enid for the Oklahoma 2-Year-Old Futurity trials and finals.

In her division of the trials, Mona Leta woke up the whole Quarter Horse racing world by sprinting the 220-yard distance in :12.2 and establishing a new 2-year-old world record.

In the finals, she covered the distance in the same lightning-fast time. Still, she was not immediately declared the winner.

"In the futurity finals," Walter says, "all of the track stewards were standing up off the ground, in an observation booth.

"As the horses sprinted past them and neared the finish line, they all had their eyes fixed firmly on the pack. They didn't even notice Mona Leta because she wasn't anywhere near the pack. She was way out in front of it.

"So, after the race was over, they declared the second-place horse the winner. The crowd started booing, so they waited for the photo finish. They saw that they'd made a little mistake and presented the winner's trophy to Mona Leta."

It was also at Enid that Mona Leta was shown in her first, and last, halter class.

"By this time," says Walter, "Tien and me had become good friends with Dorothy and Ed Cox, Mr. H. S. Bissell's daughter and son-in-law.

"They came up from Las Cruces and went to the futurity with us. On the day after Mona Leta won the finals, there was a horse show with halter and performance classes. Dorothy talked me into entering 'Mona' in the 2-year-old filly class.

"I let Ed lead her in the class. I can't even remember who the judge was that day, or exactly how he placed Mona. I just know it was way down there.

"Well, Dorothy got a little agitated and went up to him the first chance she got and asked him what he didn't like about the filly.

" 'I just didn't like the way she moved,' was all he could come up with.

" 'Well,' Dorothy said, 'she moved well enough yesterday to win the futurity and set a world's record!' "

Regardless of her lack of prowess in the Enid halter ring, Mona Leta made a good enough impression on John Batson of Marietta, Oklahoma, to prompt him to offer $3,500 for her.

Walter accepted, with the proviso that he remain in control of the speedy filly until after the Rocky Mountain Quarter Horse Association's (RMQHA) 2-year-old futurity, to be run at Centennial Park race track, on the outskirts of Denver, in 3½ weeks.

Entered in the trials of the 330-yard RMQHA Futurity (now known as the Mile High Futurity) on August 30, 1951, Mona Leta breezed to victory over two other Leo offspring—Robin Reed and Leolita. In the finals several days later, she again emerged victorious, with her winning time of :17.0 establishing a track record and a 2-year-old world record.

Still under Walter's care and training, Mona was next entered in the New Mexico State Fair race meet in Albuquerque. There, on October 5, she was entered in a winner-take-all event for 2-year-olds.

The fleet bay Leo and Hot Heels daughter was undefeated to this point, as were two other highly-regarded fillies—Gold Bar, a daughter of Three Bars (TB) and Goldienug, and Miss Tacubaya, a daughter of Depth Charge (TB) and Garcia Flicka. Also entered in the race were Parker's Trouble, by Ed Echols; Leolita by Leo; and Brigand (TB) by Depth Charge. All five horses had already won major stakes events.

"Well, she moved well enough yesterday to win the futurity and set a world's record!"

The race was for 440 yards. Mona Leta broke on top and held the lead to the 200-yard mark. At that point, Gold Bar assumed command and raced to a half-length victory over Mona Leta in :22.8.

After the Albuquerque meet was over, Mona Leta was taken back to Oklahoma by Batson. Entered by him in the 1952 Oklahoma Derby at Enid, and the 1952 RMQHA Derby at Centennial, she won both events. En route to victory in the latter race, Mona Leta navigated the 440-yard distance in :22.2, equaling the 3-year-old world record held jointly by Maddon's Bright Eyes, Blob, Jr., and Tonto Bars Gill.

In recognition of her sophomore year accomplishments, the Walter Merrick-bred speedster shared honors with Black East Bunny as the 1952 World Champion Three-Year-Old Filly.

Back in Crawford, Oklahoma, Mona Leta's breeder, conditioner and trainer was once again without a sprinting superstar, and consequently was planning his next plan of attack to get one.

The course he ultimately decided upon was a risky one, and one that he would be heavily criticized for charting. But it was also one that almost immediately took his horse racing program to the forefront of the industry, and one that dramatically altered the course of Quarter Horse evolution, as well.

All that was necessary to put it in place was to nail down the use of one stallion—and then have the guts to gamble everything on him.

*After winning her trial heat, Mona Leta returned to claim victory in the finals of the 1951 RMQHA Futurity. Here, Lester Goodson and his wife present the trophy to Tien. Walter stands directly behind Mrs. Goodson.*

# 10

# A GAMBLE PAYS OFF

*"Man, I thought he was one of the best-looking studs I'd ever seen.
'I don't know who owns this horse,' I said, 'but I've got to have him.' "*
—*Walter Merrick*

THE PERMANENT loss of Midnight Jr. in early 1951 shocked Walter Merrick into the realization that, stallion-wise, his program was at a crossroads. While he was utilizing both Revenue and Monterrey as herd sires, he was not completely satisfied with either horse.

He felt he needed to inject some new blood into his racehorses that would enable them to be competitive at not only 250 or 300 yards, but at a full quarter of a mile, as well. He further felt that, to get that kind of staying power he needed to inject Thoroughbred blood.

If the truth were to be known, Walter had arrived at this decision several years prior to Midnight Jr.'s passing. And by that time he had even found a stallion who he thought would fill the bill. All that was needed was to find a way to get that stallion to Oklahoma.

"Both Midnight Jr. and Grey Badger II were great horses—up to a certain point," Walter says. "They were fast away from the gates, and fast up to 300 yards. After that, they kind of ran out of gas.

"So, in the late 1940s I began breeding some of my mares to such Thoroughbred stallions as Piggin String and Los Molinos in an attempt

to stretch my racehorses out a little bit.

"And I began to seriously search for a Thoroughbred stallion to head my program. But not just any Thoroughbred. The horse I was looking for would have to have proven early speed and he would have to have good stock horse conformation and some athletic ability. I was still a cattle rancher at heart, and I wanted to raise racehorses that I could ride. I knew that finding a horse that had all those traits was going to be hard. But I was determined."

In 1950, while at the Tucson, Arizona, rodeo fairgrounds race meet, Merrick's perseverance paid off.

"Not long after Hank Wilson and I arrived in town for the Tucson meet," he says, "we got well-acquainted with a border patrolman named R.G. Mitchelena, or 'Mitch' as he liked to be called.

"Hank and I were staying at a motel near the track, and Mitch knew about what time we would get up every morning. He'd come by and get us, and we'd go uptown and eat breakfast.

"After breakfast one morning, we were talking and I made the remark that I was kind of looking for a good Thoroughbred stud. 'Come on and get in my car,' Mitch said, 'and I'll show you one.' We drove eight miles south of Tucson to a Mexican's place.

"There was a Thoroughbred stallion standing in a corral there. Man, I thought he was one of the best-looking studs I'd ever seen. He had a beautiful head—way better than most Thoroughbreds—and a big, pretty eye. He stood 15-3 hands high and looked to weigh in the vicinity of 1,250 pounds.

"And he was beautifully balanced and had a lot of muscle. Not short, bunchy muscle like a bulldog Quarter Horse. Long, smooth muscle. The kind I liked to see.

" 'I don't know who owns this horse,' I said, 'but I've got to have him.' The Mexican wasn't home, but Mitch knew that the horse's name was Three Bars and that he was owned by a man named Sid Vail, who lived 100 miles away in Douglas, Arizona.

"I said, 'Let's call him and see if he's interested in selling.'

"So I got Sid on the phone, told him who I was, and that I'd like to buy his horse. He didn't want to sell him, so I told him I'd like to lease him, then, and that I thought I could take him back to Oklahoma and fill his book.

" 'I don't want to do anything this year,' he said. 'But I haven't been getting very many mares to him down here. If I don't get any more this season, I'll call you.'

"I could see he wasn't going to give in, so I just had to crawl back in the car and leave the horse standing in the corral."

Three Bars, the horse that had so intrigued Walter, was a 1940 chestnut stallion. Bred by James Parrish of Midway, Kentucky, he was sired by Percentage and was out of Myrtle Dee by Luke McLuke.

Percentage was a multiple stakes winner, and Myrtle Dee had once set a record for 5½ furlongs at the old Coney Island track in Cincinnati, Ohio. In addition, Luke McLuke had won the 1914 Belmont Stakes. So the Vail-owned stallion was fashionably bred.

As for his own racing ability, Three Bars had shown great promise and tremendous breakaway speed, but his early career had been plagued with circulation problems in a hind leg.

Once sold for $300, he did manage to win his maiden race as a 3-year-old at Churchill Downs in Lexington, Kentucky. As a 4-year-old, he won three of four starts before being claimed in a $2,000 claiming race in Detroit, Michigan. Toad Haggard and Stan Snedigar, his new owners, promptly hauled him to Arizona—the hotbed of Quarter Horse racing—with plans to run him and stand him at stud.

It was at this point that Sid Vail entered Three Bars' life. Vail was a former Idaho cowboy and a pioneer Quarter Horse breeder who had purchased his seed stock from such AQHA Hall of Fame horsemen as Coke Roberds and Marshall Peavy of Hayden, Colorado.

Upon hearing of Three Bars' arrival in the area, Vail initially went to look him over with the intention of breeding a couple of mares to him. He was so impressed with the 5-year-old stallion, however, that he offered $5,000 for him. That was refused, but, undaunted, Vail returned a week later and upped the ante to $10,000. That offer was accepted.

Vail arranged to stand Three Bars at Melville Haskell's Rincon Stock Farm near Tucson for the 1945 breeding season. That arrangement resulted in 11 foals in 1946, including First Bar, a record-setting Thoroughbred son, and Barred, a record-setting Quarter Horse son.

Then, in partnership with several other men, Vail returned Three Bars to the track. In 1946, the stallion won eight of 17 starts, including the Agua Caliente Speed Handicap at Tijuana, Mexico. He also set a track record for five furlongs at the Phoenix Fairground. A sore left front ankle necessitated the then-7-year-old stallion's permanent retirement in 1947, and he was returned to Haskell for the 1948 breeding season.

Still, the Arizona short-horse crowd was slow to embrace Three Bars. They were far more enamored with Piggin

"So I could see that the Three Bars horses were on the verge of exploding on the Quarter Horse racing scene."

# THREE BARS
## WILL STAND THE 1952 SEASON AT
# CRAWFORD, OKLAHOMA
## Fee $300 — With Return Privileges

Three Bars is a Thoroughbred horse by Percentage and out of Myrtle Dee by Luke McLuke. He is a Stakes winner of ten races. His best times are — one-quarter, :21.3; three-eighths, :32.3; one-half, :44.4, five-eighths, :56.4; five and one half furlongs, 1:03.2; three-quarters, 1:10.1.

He has two crops of foals of racing age. He has five register of merit qualifiers to his credit. They are BARJO, DISBARRED, GLASS BAR who set a track record at Tucson and was unbeaten as a two-year old, BARRED, the Quarter running horse of the month for April; GOLD BAR, winner of the Ruidoso Futurity and the winner-take-all for two-year-olds at Albuquerque.

Some of his winning Thoroughbred colts include PROVOCATION, FORT BARS, JOINT VENTURE, and FIRST BAR, winner of thirteen races, including the George Drumheller Memorial handicap at Longacres, beating the best two-year-olds on the West Coast. THREE BARS' colts are also winning in the show ring as well as on the race track.

### I Am Booking Now For The 1952 Season

Address All Communications To:

# Walter Merrick

**CRAWFORD,**                    **OKLAHOMA**

*Here is Walter Merrick's hallmark advertisement as it appeared in the November 1951 issue of* The Quarter Horse Journal, *announcing that he would stand Three Bars (TB) in Crawford, Oklahoma, in 1952. It was an ad and an event that altered the course of Quarter Horse evolution.*

**Courtesy** *The Quarter Horse Journal*

String, Rukin and Frances Jelks' Thoroughbred stallion who had been named the 1943-44 AQRA Co-Champion Running Stallion and the 1945-46 AQRA Champion Running Stallion.

At the time that Walter Merrick got his first glimpse of Three Bars, the stallion was 10 years old and had sired a total of one Register of Merit Quarter racehorse—Barred. Still, Merrick's eye for a horse and intuitive ability to recognize a winner led him to believe that Three Bars was the very horse he'd been searching for, and he was determined to incorporate the stallion's blood into his Oklahoma breeding program.

"I was pretty disappointed that I couldn't talk Sid into letting me take Three Bars back with me to Oklahoma after the Tucson meet," he says. "But I didn't forget about him. Not by a long shot.

"Van Smelker, who was running the AQHA racing program back then, used to pick a Quarter Running Horse of the Month and put it in *The Quarter Horse Journal*. In April of 1951, he chose Barred.

"I was running Mona Leta that year, and the first time she got beat was when Gold Bars, Three Bars' first great running daughter, beat her in the 2-year-old winner-take-all race at Albuquerque.

"And Barjo and Tonto Bars Gill were two more Three Bars 2-year-old colts who won big that year. All four horses qualified for their AA ratings and went on to be AAA runners when they came up with that classification.

"So I could see that the Three Bars horses were on the verge of exploding on the Quarter Horse racing scene. And I was more determined than ever to get a piece of the action."

That fall, Merrick's resolve was rewarded.

"In September of 1951," he says, "Sid gave me a call. He hadn't gotten very many mares to Three Bars the previous spring, and he was ready to do business. Tien and I were on our way to the New Mexico State Fair race meet with Mona Leta, so Sid agreed to drive up and meet with me.

"When we got together, he said, 'I'll lease Three Bars to you, but I want to breed 10 mares to him.'

" 'I'll make you a deal,' I said. 'I'll stand the horse for two years in Crawford. You bring however many mares you want. I'll breed them, but then I want to breed an equal number of my mares for free. I'll stand him for $300 and we'll split that money right down the middle.' He agreed, and we shook hands on it."

Early the next year, Vail delivered Three Bars and 10 mares to the Merrick Ranch. That meant that Walter had 10 breedings coming.

The Oklahoma horseman was elated, and his enthusiasm was contagious. It didn't take long for the Mountains and Plains racing fraternity to respond to his call to come look at, and breed to, the "new kid in town."

Walter thinks it was the carelessness of one of those potential customers, though, who gave him quite a scare.

"During the breeding season," he says, "someone stopped by to look at Three Bars when we weren't home.

"I had built two big, concrete box stalls with attached stud runs onto the east end of my barn. I kept Three Bars in one and Monterrey in the other. And there was a little space between them so they couldn't get at each other.

"Whoever came to the place apparently went into Three Bars' pen. After they were done looking at him, they left. The only problem was, they left the gate to his run open.

"Well, Three Bars had never been in a horse fight in his life, but Monterrey was a range stud and he knew all about fighting. Three Bars must have went over to Monterrey's pen to check him out. As near as I can figure, Monterrey grabbed Three Bars by the right nostril and just flat ripped half of it off.

"When I got home, there Three Bars stood with half his right nostril just

"By the time the breeding season was over, I'd bred Three Bars to 70 mares."

hanging by a thread. I guess I should have called a vet, but we were a long ways from town. So I just got my pocketknife out and trimmed the loose piece off. He healed up OK, but from that day on, his right nostril was just half the size of his left one."

Cosmetic flaw notwithstanding, and just as Walter had predicted he would, Merrick's leased stallion stood to a full book of mares in 1952. And it was a book that was handled through hand-breeding and live cover only.

"By the time the breeding season was over," Walter says, "I'd bred Three Bars to 70 mares—10 each for Sid and me, and 50 outside mares. Most of them were Quarter Horses, but there were a few Thoroughbreds, as well. And they were owned by some of the top racehorse men in the region. I felt for sure that we'd get some good-looking runners as a result."

As Merrick, Vail and their customers awaited what would be Three Bars' biggest foal crop to date, the stallion's 1950 crop hit the track in 1952. Represented by only 12 foals, and nine race performers, Three Bars sired six AAA-rated runners.

Bardella, a sorrel mare out of Della P. by Doc Horn, was the cream of the crop. The winner of four futurities and stakes races, she set or equaled two track records and was named the 1952 World Champion Two-Year-Old Filly.

In addition, Tonto Bars Gill, now a sophomore runner, had hit his full stride. The winner of four stakes events, he set two track records and was named the 1952 World Champion Three-Year-Old Colt.

The Three Bars horses were gaining momentum, and the following year was simply a repeat performance.

Leading the pack of the 1951 foals that hit the track in 1953 was Josie's Bar. A sorrel mare out of Josephine R. by Raffles (TB), she would earn a AAA rating and set a track record as a 2-year-old. She would then go on the following year to win five stakes races, set or equal six more track records, and be named the 1954 World Champion, World Champion Mare and World Champion Three-Year-Old Filly.

Although he never owned her, Walter Merrick was instrumental in Josie's Bar's rise to stardom.

"In the summer of 1951," he said, "Oscar Cox and I had hauled some horses to a race meet in Temple, Oklahoma. The man who owned the track was named James Reece, and he kept some of his mares and foals on the grounds.

"There was a Thoroughbred-looking mare in the bunch that I later found out was named Josephine R. She had a really nice filly at her side. I asked around and found out that the filly was sired by Three Bars. I told Oscar that I thought he should try to buy the filly. He looked up Reece and got the deal done. After the meet was over, we just loaded that filly up with our racehorses and hauled her home.

"Oscar named her Josie's Bar, and he owned her when she won her three world championships."

As good as she was, Josie's Bar was far from the only star from the 1951 Three Bars foal crop.

Miss Myrna Bar, a sorrel mare out of Miss Myrna by Chicaro Bill, won four futurities and stakes races, set or equaled three track records, and was the 1953 World Champion Two-Year-Old Filly.

Lightning Bar, a sorrel full brother to Bardella, earned a AAA rating on the track and an AQHA Championship in the show ring. Sugar Bars, a sorrel stallion out of Frontera Sugar by Rey, also earned a AAA rating. Both stallions then went on to become legendary sires in their own right.

In addition, Bar Annie, De Witt Bar, Deep Water and Wonder Bar all achieved AAA ratings.

At home on the Merrick Ranch in the spring of 1953, the eagerly-awaited first Sooner State crop of Three Bars foals began hitting the ground. By the time the foaling season was over, Walter found himself in the possession of 10 of the best-looking prospects he'd ever raised.

"That first crop of foals was something," he says. "I had bred

**Leading the pack of the [Three Bars] foals that hit the track in 1953 was Josie's Bar.**

*Although he never owned Josie's Bar, Walter did locate the Three Bars daughter for Oscar Cox of Lawton, Oklahoma. While owned by Cox, Josie's Bar was the 1954 World Champion Running Horse.*

Three Bars to the best mares I owned, and they sure nicked with him. There were two black colts and a sorrel filly in the bunch, and they were by far the best foals I'd ever raised. As far as I was concerned, the only bad thing about the whole experience was that it was going to be two years before I could see how fast those foals could run."

As far as Walter was concerned, everything was proceeding according to plan. That fall, he began preparing for the upcoming 1953 breeding season. Then his master plan suffered a major setback.

"One Saturday in the fall of 1952," Walter says, "Sid drove into my yard. He said he had come to pick Three Bars up. 'Sid,' I said, 'that wasn't the deal. We agreed that I'd have the use of him for two seasons.

" 'Yeah, I know,' he said. 'But there's a lot of folks wanting to breed to him down in Arizona, and I think I can make a go of it now.' We argued about it a little, then went in and had supper. Sid stayed at my place that night.

"The next morning—Sunday—he got up early and went out to load Three Bars.

"We messed around a little and took some pictures. Then I said to him, 'Sid, what'll it cost me for you to leave the horse here? What'll it take to buy him?'

" 'Fifty-thousand dollars,' he said.

" 'OK,' I replied, 'I'll take him. But I'll need until Tuesday or Wednesday to round up the money.' John Hanson, my friend from North Platte, Nebraska, was a wealthy man. I was sure I could talk him into backing me.

" 'Nope,' Sid said, 'I need the money now—today—or I'm loading him up.'

"Well, there was no way I could get anything done on Sunday, so I had to let him load Three Bars up and leave. We'd shook hands on a two-year lease, but we never put anything in writing, so there wasn't much I could do about it."

Despite the fact that he'd had his guaranteed use of Three Bars cut in half, Walter still had an outstanding

**'Sid, what'll it cost me for you to leave the horse here? What'll it take to buy him?'**

set of young prospects by him that were fast approaching the time when he could begin conditioning them for the track.

As the Merrick-bred Three Bars foals progressed through their yearling year, another crop of Three Bars freshmen runners worked their magic on the Quarter Horse straightaways. This crop, born in 1952, numbered only 11. Still, it produced the AAA-rated War Chant, Rocket Bar (the gelding), Iron Bars, La Bar and Pinch Bar, and the AA-rated Skylark Bar, Anna Bar, Bar's Bar and Panola Bar.

Finally, it was time for the class of '53 to show what they could do. It was an impressive class, and standing at its head was a black colt named Bob's Folly.

"Back in June of 1953," Walter says, "when my Three Bars horses were weanlings, I held my fourth Quarter Horse sale. I had enough horses at the time to put it on myself, and as a highlight I consigned Hot Heels and her black Three Bars colt as lot Number 1.

"I also put Wampus Cat and Tidy M. in the sale. Wampus Cat was a daughter of Revenue and Jean Marie, and she had a nice sorrel Three Bars filly at her side. Tidy M. was the Grey Badger II mare I'd gotten from Oscar, and she was heavy in foal to Three Bars. I guess I sold two or three more Three Bars foals in the sale, and because I had Three Bars leased for the 1954 breeding season, I also sold Monterrey.

"But Hot Heels and her colt were the feature attraction, and they topped the sale. A doctor from Hugoton, Kansas, named R.T. LeNeve bought them for $7,000.

"After the sale was over, I was visiting with him and said, 'Doctor, what are you going to do with that colt?'

" 'I don't know,' he said. 'I haven't given it much thought.'

" 'Well,' I said, 'If you ever decide to run him, I'd like to have a chance at training him.'

"The doctor loaded the mare and colt up, and I didn't hear from him

*These shots of Walter Merrick and Three Bars were taken in the fall of 1952, on the day that Sid Vail picked Three Bars up for the stallion's return to Arizona.*

again for almost two years. Then he gave me a call and told me he'd like to bring the colt—he'd named him Bob's Folly—down for me to train and race.

"By this time," Walter continues, "I was keeping my race prospects down at the fairgrounds in Sayre, Oklahoma. It was around 45 miles south of the ranch.

"I had a young man named Ted Wells, from Pawhuska, Oklahoma, helping me with the training. He went on to become a top race trainer, and won the 1965 All-American Futurity in Ruidoso with Savannah Jr.

"I also had a boy by the name of Emil Armstrong who lived with me in Crawford. In the summer, he'd stay down in Sayre, too, in a trailer I kept down there, and help work the horses.

"In the fall of 1955, I sent Ted and the Three Bars 2-year-olds up to the Centennial meet in Denver. I was obligated to take a group of

*Here's Hot Heels, Walter's home-bred daughter of Midnight Jr. and Joan, with her 1953 black Three Bars colt. The good-looking pair were the feature attraction of Walter's 1953 production sale and sold for $7,000 to Dr. R. T. LeNeve of Hugoton, Kansas.*

*Hot Heels' colt, named Bob's Folly, was returned to Walter as a 2-year-old to be trained and raced. Emil Armstrong is aboard 'Bob' in this 1956 shot taken at Albuquerque, right after the black stallion set a 440-yard world record.*

Thoroughbreds to run at the Ak-Sar-Ben meet in Omaha, Nebraska, so Tien and I headed up there.

"The Ak-Sar-Ben races were run during the early afternoon and the Centennial races were run at night. As often as we could, Tien and I would run our horses in Omaha and then hop on an airplane and fly to Denver to watch the Three Bars colts run at Centennial."

Although he entrusted a number of top race prospects to young Wells, Walter opted to keep the top prospect with him.

"By the time I left for Ak-Sar-Ben," he says, "I knew Bob's Folly was the best of the bunch. I'd run him in the Pawhuska Futurity in Pawhuska, Oklahoma, and he'd won his trial heat and the finals with no sweat. There weren't any Quarter Horse races at the Omaha meet, but I still didn't want that colt out of my control.

"He was entered in the Kansas Futurity," he continues, "and it was going to be run at Centennial after the Ak-Sar-Ben meet was over. Toward the end of the meet, I figured I should try to breeze 'Bob' out at least once. So, one morning I had my jockey take him over to work out of the gates.

"There were some other horses being worked, too, so as each rider and horse approached the gates, the starter would ask the rider who the horse was.

"As my jockey and Bob's Folly got to the gate, the starter asked, 'What have you got there, jock?' 'I don't know,' my jockey said. 'Walt didn't tell me the name of this horse.' " 'Well, you tell Walt not to do that again,' he said.

"But he let the horse get loaded into the gate and got him and the other horses off. Bob just busted out of there and walked off and left those Thoroughbreds.

"I was standing under the steward's stand, watching the horses work, and there was a group of men up in the stands who were watching them, too.

"I heard one of them say, 'Lordy, look at that black colt run! Whose horse is that?'

*(Above) As the crowning achievement of his brilliant freshman campaign, Bob's Folly won the all-ages RMQHA Stallion Stakes, run in August 1955 at Centennial.*

*(Left) Walter and Bob's Folly strike a pose on the track at Ruidoso Downs, New Mexico.* **Top photo by Ralph Morgan. Bottom photo by Trans-Photo Laboratories**

*Lady K Bars, a 1953 sorrel mare by Three Bars and out of Chubby Reed, was a AAA-rated runner who earned $8,660 in an era of low purses. Merrick protégé Emil Armstrong is up on the beautiful mare in this shot.*

" 'I don't know,' said another man, 'But I can tell you one thing. He hasn't run here before.'

"After the workout was over, I went to take Bob back to the barn. The second man, who was black and a top race steward, followed me. I just knew I was in trouble.

"But all he said was, 'Mr. Walt, are you planning on running that colt anywhere?'

" 'Yes I am,' I said. 'I'm gonna run him at Denver next week.'

" 'Here's two dollars,' he said. 'The first time you run this colt, you just put this money right down on his nose. To win.'

"I wound up racing Bob's Folly for three seasons. We won the Kansas and RMQHA futurities in Denver, and then I entered him in the all-age RMQHA Stallion Stakes. People

criticized me for running a 2-year-old colt against older horses, but I knew Bob's Folly was up to it. It was a 440-yard race, and we won it and beat such world champion horses as Ridge Butler and Rukin String in the process.

"As a 3-year-old, he won eight stakes races and Bob set a world's record for 440 yards—breaking the one that had been set years earlier by Woven Web. The only horse we couldn't beat was Go Man Go. He was the same age as Bob, and if he hadn't been, our horse would have been the 2- and 3-year-old champion for sure.

"I'll probably get accused of being prejudiced when I say this, but I feel to this very day that Bob's Folly was the fastest son of Three Bars."

Although Bob's Folly was the acknowledged star of the Merrick-

*Tidy Bar, a 1953 gray gelding by Three Bars and out of Tidy M. by Grey Badger II, was another top Merrick runner. AAA-rated, he is shown here after winning a 400-yard sprint on October 4, 1957, at the New Mexico State Fair race meet in Albuquerque. Elbert Minchey is the jockey.*

**Photo by Trans-Photo Laboratories**

*Hickory Red (TB), a 1953 sorrel stallion by Three Bars and out of Copper Lady, was unable to race until he was a 4-year-old due to injury. He won his maiden race—the Joe Reilly Purse—as a 90-to-1 longshot.*

**Photo by Trans-Photo Laboratories**

bred Three Bars racing string, there were other headliners, as well.

Lady K Bar, a beautiful blazed-face, stocking-legged sorrel mare out of Chubby Reed by Chubby, earned her AAA rating, and Tidy Bar, a gray gelding out of Tidy M. by Grey Badger II, did the same. And three Merrick-bred Three Bars Thoroughbreds—Roger Mills, Chapparita and Hickory Red—were all winners, as well. Of the latter trio, Chapparita and Hickory Red were the Merrick favorites.

"Chapparita was just a slender little mare," Walter says. "She didn't have very good conformation and hardly any muscle at all. But she was pure poison as a runner. We raced her for several years and she was tough to beat.

"Hickory Red, on the other hand, was a good-looking horse. He was out

of a mare named Copper Lady, and she was Man 'O War-bred. For some reason, Tien took a real shine to Hickory Red. She used to tell everybody, 'This is my colt.' So I just put him in her name.

"I put 'Hickory' in training with the rest of my Three Bars 2-year-olds, but he was kind of a hard-luck colt. It just seemed like I couldn't keep him sound. As a result, I never got a chance to start him until 1957, when he was a 4-year-old.

"Then I entered him in a stakes race—the Joe Reilly Purse—at Ruidoso Downs. Here he was, a 4-year-old who had never been in a race, competing against seasoned stakes winners. He went off as a 90-to-1 longshot.

"I guess I didn't have enough faith in him to bet on him, but Tien sure did. She put $20 on him to win. Well,

'Hickory' just ran off and hid from the rest of the field. He beat 'em by at least four lengths and Tien collected $1,800 at the pay window. She was walking on clouds for a while after that."

In addition to the Merrick-Three Bars Quarter Horse and Thoroughbred racehorses, the class of 1953 produced a world champion halter stallion, as well.

"I had re-acquired Joan, my original Burnett Ranch mare, in the fall of 1951," Walter says. "So, naturally, I bred her to Three Bars in 1952. She had a beautiful black colt the following year, who I named Steel Bars.

"When the colt was around 4 months old, Joan came down with lockjaw. I took her to the vet and he tried to save her but couldn't. The colt was old enough to be weaned, though, so he got along fine.

"In the early summer of 1955," he continues, "B.F. Phillips of Frisco, Texas, and his trainer, Matlock Rose, came up to look at my Three Bars horses. They were in the market for a

young stud prospect. They took a shine to Steel Bars and asked me to price him. So I did. I told them I'd take $10,000 for him. They studied on it for a while, and then left without him.

"Later on in the fall, B.F. called me and said, 'Walter, I've decided to buy your black colt. I'll send a man up after him.'

" 'He'll have to drive a little farther to pick him up,' I said. 'I've got him up in Denver at the racetrack.' 'Oh, hell,' he said. 'Call up there and tell them to quit training him. I don't want anything to do with any racehorses.'

"Well, B.F. eventually changed his mind about racehorses. He went on to own and race some of the best, including Dash For Cash. But he wanted Steel Bars as a halter horse and the colt made him a real good one. In fact, he was the 1957 AQHA High-Point Halter Stallion."

All in all, Walter Merrick's Three Bars experience was a positive one. And one of monumental import. At

*Walter sold Steel Bars, a 1953 black stallion by Three Bars and out of Joan, to B. F. Phillips of Frisco, Texas. Steel Bars went on to become the first Quarter Horse stallion to be named grand champion in Fort Worth, San Antonio and Houston in the same year. He is shown here after earning Grand Champion Stallion honors at the 1956 Texas State Fair in Dallas.*

*Photo by Ray Davis, courtesy* Western Horseman *magazine*

*Bar Bob, a 1953 sorrel stallion by Three Bars and out of Della Bob by Leo, was a AAA-rated racehorse, an AQHA Champion, and the earner of 32 halter and five performance points. He went on to become a top sire of racehorses, halter and performance horses.*

**Photo by Dalco, courtesy**
*The Quarter Horse Journal*

the time the Oklahoma racehorse man discovered the stallion in a corral south of Tucson, the horse was a regional entity at best.

Would he have gone on to become a national celebrity without Walter's involvement? Probably. Would he have risen as fast, and become as universally popular? Probably not.

The service Walter rendered Three Bars, therefore, was invaluable.

Walter Merrick, with his tremendous eye for a horse, took a look at a relatively unknown Thoroughbred stallion and realized he was viewing perfection. This was the one horse, he reasoned, who could sire not only speed, but flawless Quarter Horse conformation as well.

And, because of his stature as a horseman, Walter was able to convince such die-hard Quarter Horse purists as Bud Warren of Perry, Oklahoma, and R.H. Patterson of Emmett, Idaho, to breed their Leo mares to Three Bars. These were the first two such matches in what would go on to become one of the greatest "golden crosses" of all time.

The results of just those two 1953 Three Bars-Leo crosses—Leo Bar and Bar Bob—would go on to write several chapters of Quarter Horse history by themselves.

But, more importantly than just the proving of one cross, the Walter Merrick-Three Bars venture served notice to the entire Quarter Horse world that there was a Thoroughbred stallion who could sire both a 440-yard world-record holder—like Bob's Folly—and an AQHA honor roll halter stallion—like Steel Bars—out of foundation-bred, bulldog Quarter Horse mares.

As a result, Three Bars' popularity soared, and people began hauling not only race mares, but halter and working mares to him, as well. The resulting foals began to dominate virtually every field of organized Quarter Horse competition.

The course of Quarter Horse evolution had been forever altered. The era of the bulldog horse was ended. In its stead was the era of the taller, more versatile athlete; the age of the AQHA Supreme Champion.

As was to be expected, it was a transition that was not immediately embraced by all.

"There were a lot of people who criticized me for using Three Bars," Walter says. "They'd corner me at the AQHA conventions and at horse shows, and say, 'Walter, you're trying to ruin the Quarter Horse breed with your half-breds.'

" 'I'm not trying to ruin anything,' I'd tell 'em. 'I'm just trying to raise my kind of horses. And so are you boys. So you just go on raising horses that suit you and I'll do the same.' "

And most of the horses that suited Walter from that point on would have that one Thoroughbred stallion's name in their pedigree. The first chapter of the Walter Merrick-Three Bars story was complete, but there were still several more monumental ones to be written.

*Leo Bar, a 1953 sorrel stallion by Three Bars and out of Flit by Leo, was bred by Bud Warren of Perry, Oklahoma. A AAA-rated racehorse and the sire of AAA runners and AQHA champions, he also went on to become an influential sire.*

**Courtesy**
***The Quarter Horse Journal***

# 11 IT'S IN THE BLOOD

*"Boys, we've got a little problem that we need to take care of.
There's a Thoroughbred mare who owns all of our world's records,
and we can't have that."*
*—Bud Warren*

*Lena Valenti (TB), the
founding matriarch of
a great line of Quarter
racehorses, is shown
here after winning
a 3/8th-mile race at
Arnett, Oklahoma, in
May of 1951. Then-
owner Eldon Cluck of
Dumas, Texas, is at the
stocky mare's head.*
**Photo by Foto Flash**

AS THE 1953 breeding season drew near, Walter Merrick again found himself in the unenviable position of being without a resident herd sire.

His June 1953 sale had reduced his mare numbers, so this wouldn't loom as an insurmountable problem. And with the sale not occurring until June 24, there was enough time to get a couple of mares safely in foal to Monterrey.

Still, it was Three Bars who dominated Walter's thinking. The stallion might have been spirited away to Southern Arizona, but that didn't mean he was out of the picture. Walter was determined to wind up with a Three Bars-bred stud of his own—one that no one could take away from him without his consent.

As does every true horse breeder, Walter knew how important it was for any potential breeding stallion to have a top-notch "stud's mother" for a

dam. In 1953, Walter felt he had just the mare to fill that bill.

"Back in 1951," he says, "Eldon Cluck of Dumas, Texas, brought a typey little Thoroughbred mare to me, to train and campaign on the track. Her name was Lena Valenti, and she was a 1946 bay mare sired by Gray Dream and out of Perhobo by Percentage.

"Gray Dream was a well-known sire of early speed in this country, and Percentage was the sire of Three Bars.

"Anyway, I raced Lena Valenti for Eldon and got along real well with her. I ran her mainly on the Thoroughbred tracks, at shorter distances. But one time, at a meet in Enid in August 1951, they needed some horses to fill a 440-yard Quarter Horse race. They came to me and asked if I had any horses I could put in the race. I had a lot of faith in 'Lena's' early speed, so I entered her.

*Lena's Bar (TB), a 1954 chestnut mare by Three Bars and out of Lena Valenti, was a top performer on the straightaway tracks. She is shown here with trainer Ted Wells Jr. and jockey Elbert Minchey after a victory in a 1961 400-yard contest at Sunland Park, New Mexico.*

In what was arguably her greatest race –the 1959 Miller Motel Allowance at Ruidoso Downs, Lena's Bar defeated four world champions and one Honor Roll racehorse.

**Photo by Trans-Photo Lab**

"This was right before the AQRA consolidated with the AQHA, and shortly before they made a AAA race rating. So the race was run under AQRA rules and AA was the highest rating a horse could get. Lena won the race and got her AA, Register of Merit rating that day."

Several years later, Eldon offered Walter a broodmare package deal that he couldn't refuse.

"Eldon told me he had two mares he'd consider selling," Walter says. "One was a Thoroughbred match race mare named Miss Derrick and the other was Lena Valenti.

"I knew the Miss Derrick mare. I wasn't too keen about buying her but I really wanted Lena. Eldon wouldn't separate the pair, though, so I had to take 'em both. Then I resold Miss Derrick."

In 1952, Walter opted to breed Lena Valenti to Three Bars. She failed to settle, however, so he hauled her to Arizona the next year and to have her re-bred. The second try was successful, with the result being a 1954 chestnut Thoroughbred filly named Lena's Bar.

"Lena's Bar wasn't a big mare," Walter says, "but she was a well-made, pretty thing. I broke her to ride as a 2-year-old, but didn't start conditioning her for the track until she was 3.

"After the AQHA took over Quarter Horse racing, about the only state where you could race Thoroughbreds in approved Quarter Horse competition was New Mexico. And even there, you couldn't run them in any futurities. So I didn't start Lena's Bar until she was 3."

Over the course of the next four racing seasons—from 1957 through 1960—the Walter Merrick-bred straight Thoroughbred daughter of Three Bars made up for having to skip her 2-year-old year of competition by becoming a one-mare wrecking crew.

In 1957, she achieved her AAA rating and equaled the 400-yard track record at Albuquerque. The next year, she won the 440-yard Buttons and Bows Stakes and the 440-yard C.L.

Maddon Bright Eyes Handicap at Albuquerque, and set a track record for 300 yards at Sunland Park. In 1959, as a 5-year-old, she won the Bright Eyes Stakes at Ruidoso Downs.

Also in 1959, Lena's Bar ran what was arguably her greatest race. The occasion was the Miller Motel Allowance, a 400-yard event held August 16 at Ruidoso Downs.

In that one race, the Merrick-bred speedster defeated four world champion Quarter Horse runners. Finishing second to her was the good AAA-rated stakes-winning mare Tidy Too. Third place went to the legendary Go Man Go—the three-time reigning AQHA World Champion Quarter Running Horse and the one horse who Lena's older half-brother, Bob's Folly, had been unable to best in eight tries.

Finishing behind Go Man Go was the world champion runner Double Bid, and he was followed closely by Easter Rose, a Walter Merrick-bred AQHA Honor Roll racehorse. Finally, behind "Rose" came Vandy's Flash and Vanetta Dee—both world champions and both by Vandy and out of Garrett's Miss Pawhuska by Leo.

All in all, it was a star-studded field and one that any racehorse owner would be proud to have bested.

Lena's Bar's final tally reveals that she went to the post 76 times, winning 24 races, finishing second 18 times, and third 10 times. Her earnings amounted to $28,311 and she was an AQHA Superior racehorse.

Getting back to Lena Valenti, in 1954 Walter chose to breed her to Leo. The following spring, she had a colt that he named Valleo. While not a top racehorse, he was campaigned as a 2-year-old and earned his racing ROM.

Back on the Merrick Ranch in 1955, Walter was still without a permanent herd sire. He did, however, wind up with the use of Iron Bars, a AAA-rated son of Three Bars, and Clovis Champ, a AAA-rated grandson of Flying Bob.

Iron Bars, who Walter had raced the year before for owner Oscar Dodson of Chillicothe, Texas, was probably the better of the two horses. Still, not wanting to hazard a half-brother-half-

In that one race, the Merrick-bred speedster defeated four world champion Quarter Horse runners.

Clovis' Doll, a 1956 bay mare by Clovis' Champion, was Lena Valenti's second foal. Shown here as a yearling, "Doll" went on to become a AAA-rated racehorse and the dam of two AAA runners, two AQHA Champions, and the earners of five Superior halter and performance awards.

As a racehorse, Clovis' Win, a 1965 sorrel gelding by Win Or Lose and out of Clovis' Doll, achieved a speed index of 95. As a show horse, he was an Open and Youth AQHA Champion, an Open and Youth Superior Halter Horse, and the earner of 225 halter and 36 performance points.

sister cross, he opted to breed Lena Valenti to Clovis Champ.

The result was Clovis' Doll, an extremely well-made 1956 sorrel mare who qualified for her AAA rating in 1958.

After Iron Bars' and Clovis Champ's one-year tour of stud duty, Bob's Folly became the focal point of the Merrick racehorse breeding program. Walter stood the stallion for R.T. LeNeve for five seasons—from 1957 through 1961—and bred most of his own mares to him each year.

It was an arrangement that, from time to time, hit a few rough spots.

"They tell me Dr. LeNeve was a fine physician up in Hugoton," Walter says. "And I can sure believe that, because he was a pretty smart man. But every now and again he'd go to drinking and get to being a little tough to be around.

"One spring, he'd had a few drinks up in Hugoton and decided he was going to come down to my place and pick Bob's Folly up and take him home. That kinda put me in a bind. I had a lot of outside mares booked to him, and my own mares to breed, as well.

"So, I did the only thing I felt I could. I had a couple of drinks in Crawford and drove up to LeNeve's place and brought Bob's Folly back.

"Before he passed away a few years ago, the doctor came down to visit Tien and me, and we all made our peace. So that was good."

In 1957, Walter decided to take a chance on the same type of brother and sister cross that he had refrained from making two years earlier. He bred Lena Valenti to Bob's Folly and came up with Roman Bob, a 1958 sorrel gelding.

"Roman Bob was probably one of the best-looking colts I ever raised," Walter says. "I raced him for a couple of years and he turned out to be a good AAA runner. In 1962, I ran him up in Colorado, at the fall meet at Centennial. After it was over, I hired a cross-country hauler to take him and my other racehorse to the Los Alamitos meet in California.

*Roman Bob, a 1958 sorrel gelding by Bob's Folly and out of Lena Valenti, was a AAA-rated stakes winner, endowed with classic Quarter Horse conformation.*

**Photo by Gene Wilson Studio**

*Here is another shot of Roman Bob, whose race career and life was cut short as a result of being stranded in a cross-country van for several days during a Colorado blizzard.*

"The van broke down in a snowstorm at the top of the Continental Divide and was stranded there for several days. Roman Bob wound up catching pneumonia and dying. But he was one of the good ones. I guess I must have had a reason for gelding him, but for the life of me I can't remember what it was."

By 1959, Sid Vail had moved from Arizona to Apple Valley, California. That spring, Walter hauled Lena Valenti out to the coast to be bred to Three Bars for the second and last time. The result was a diminutive sorrel filly named Little Lena Bars. Although, again, a straight Thoroughbred by breeding, she was unquestionably one of the fastest Quarter racehorses of all time.

"After what Lena's Bar had accomplished on the track," Walter says, "I didn't see how Little Lena Bars could ever measure up. But I put her in race training as a 3-year-old. It didn't take long for me to figure out that I wasn't going to have to worry about her spending any time in the shadow of her big sister."

In her freshman year on the track, Little Lena Bars won three stakes races—the C.L. Maddon Bright Eyes Handicap and the Shue Fly Stakes at Albuquerque, and the Captain Dick Handicap at La Mesa Park in Raton, New Mexico. In addition, she set a new world's record for 330 yards, a new La Mesa track record for 440 yards, and equaled the La Mesa track record for 400 yards.

In 1964, her sophomore year on the track, the Merrick-bred sprinter literally re-wrote the AQHA racing record books. The site of her assaults was La Mesa Park, and the occasion was a series of races billed as the All-Distance Quarter Horse Championship Series.

The barrage began on July 19, 1964. In a winning 330-yard effort, Little Lena Bars established a new world's record time of :16.6. Two weeks later, on August 2, she was entered in a 300-yard sprint. The result was the same: another win in a new world's record time of :15.4. Two weeks later, on

August 16, it was the same. A 250-yard sprint, a win, and a new world's record time of :13.3.

And the pattern continued.

On August 30, Little Lena Bars was entered in the fourth race in the series. The distance was different—220 yards—but the result was the same. Another win, in the world record-equaling time of :12.1.

On September 13, the Merrick speedster was entered in a 220-yard sprint that was not a part of the All-Distance series. There, her sterling effort was good enough to eclipse her 220-mark of two weeks earlier and establish a new world's record for the distance of 12 seconds flat.

The final Little Lena Bars-LaMesa tally was as follows: Eight weeks, five races, four world records set and one equaled. Something had to give.

"At the time Little Lena Bars was breaking all those records," Walter says, "Bud Warren was the chairman of the AQHA racing committee and I was a member of it.

"In the spring of 1965, the AQHA convention was in Fort Worth. I attended it and sat in on the racing session. Bud called the meeting to order and began his opening remarks by saying, 'Boys, we've got a little problem that we need to take care of. There's a Thoroughbred mare who owns all our world's records, and we can't have that.'

"Well, I knew who he was talking about and I knew what was going to happen. So I just excused myself and left the room. Later on, I asked one of the other committee members what they had decided to do.

"The long and short of it was that they did away with recognizing world's records. Their reasoning was that there were too many variables that went into a world's record that they had no control over. Things like irregular timing procedures on non pari-mutuel tracks.

"To be honest, I guess I could see their point. There were some tracks that really wanted all their times recognized, but just weren't up to snuff when it came to regulating the

"It didn't take long for me to figure out that I wasn't going to have to worry about her (Little Lena Bars) spending any time in the shadow of her big sister."

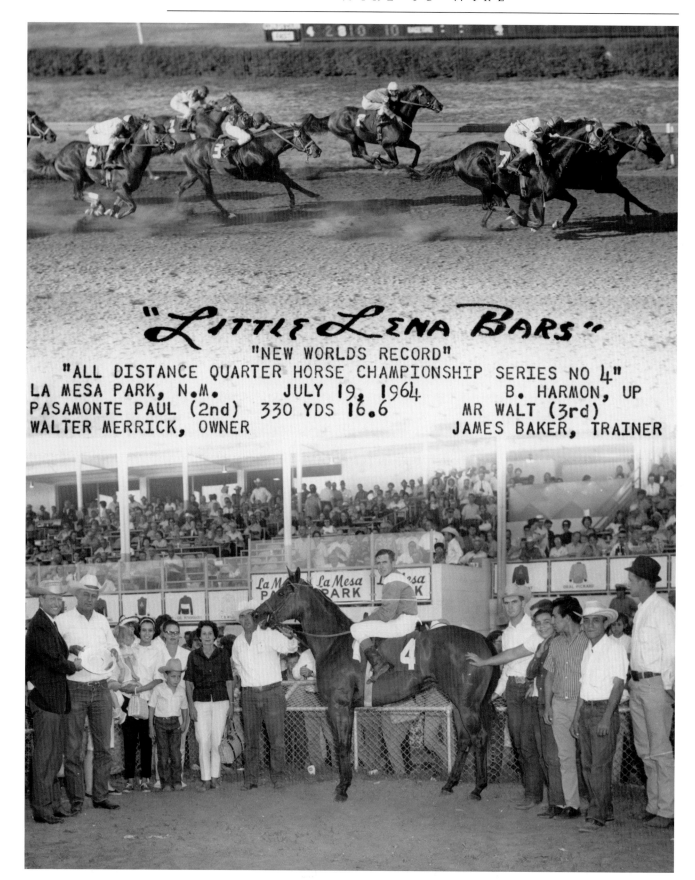

*This is Little Lena Bars (TB), a 1960 bay mare by Three Bars and out of Lena Valenti. Within a two-month span at La Mesa Park in Raton, New Mexico, in the late summer and early fall of 1964, the Merrick-bred speedster set or tied five world records. In this photo, she eclipses the 330-yard mark.*

"Little Lena Bars"

"ALL DISTANCE QUARTER HORSE CHAMPIONSHIP SERIES NUMBER 5"
LA MESA PARK, N.M.          AUG 2, 1964          BOBBY HARMON, UP
FLYING CHARGER (2nd)        300 Yds 15.4         PASAMONTE PAUL (3rd)
WALTER MERRICK, OWNER                            JAMES M. BAKER, TR.
                    "NEW WORLDS RECORD"

*In the ensuing six weeks, Little Lena Bars established new world records for 300 and 250 yards, and equaled the world record for 220 yards.*

"Little Lena Bars"

"ALL DISTANCE QUARTER HORSE CHAMPIONSHIP SERIES #6"
LA MESA PARK, N.M.          AUG. 16, 1964        B. HARMON, UP
PASAMONTE PAUL (2nd)        250 Yds 13.3         DEEP BOB (3rd)
WALTER MERRICK, OWNER    (WORLDS RECORD)    JAMES M. BAKER, TRAINER

"Little Lena Bars"

ALL DISTANCE QUARTER HORSE CHAMPIONSHIP      SERIES NO SEVEN
LA MESA PARK, N.M.          AUG. 30, 1964        B. HARMON, UP
STRAW FLIGHT (2nd)          220 YDS 12.1         MR WALT (3rd)
WALTER MERRICK, OWNER (EQUALS WORLD RECORD)   PHIL GARRETT, TRAINER

"*Little Lena Bars*"

LA MESA PARK, N.M.          SEPT 13, 1964          B. HARMON, UP
GOFAR BAR (2nd)          220 Yds :12          MR STORMY LEO (3)
WALTER MERRICK, OWNER     (NEW WORLD RECORD)     PHIL GARRETT, TR.

*Finally, on September 13, 1964, Little Lena Bars broke her own world record mark for 220 yards.*

races and reporting the results.

"But La Mesa Park wasn't one of them. There wasn't anything wrong with the way they ran their races. Bud hit the nail right on the head with his opening remarks. They just couldn't have a mare like Little Lena Bars owning all the Quarter Horse racing records."

Getting back to Lena Valenti, the dam of Merrick's two super sprinters, she wound up her broodmare career by producing two more foals.

Lena's Bobby, a 1961 chestnut mare by Bob's Folly, was unraced. Tonto's Eagle, a 1964 chestnut stallion by Tonto Bars Hank, was AA-rated.

Lena Valenti—the Thoroughbred mare who was out of Three Bars' half-sister—must go down in history as one of the premiere race producers of the Quarter Horse breed. And, through her daughters Little Lena Bars and Lena's Bar and their descendants, she continued to impact the Quarter Horse racing world in general, and the Walter Merrick breeding program in particular, for years to come.

"Countless people have asked me to tell them which of the two 'Lena's' was the fastest," Walter says.

"I never could give 'em a straight answer. They were both terrific runners, but I never worked or ran them against each other. So I guess we'll just never know which one was the fastest. But I can say one thing for sure.

"I'd like to be looking out my window at two more just like 'em today."

*Little Lena Bars—the slender Thoroughbred mare who launched one of the most devastating assaults of all time on the Quarter Horse racing record books.*

# 12

# A FEW GOOD HORSES

*"He also earned Superiors in open halter and Western pleasure, and two Superiors in youth Western pleasure. Not bad for a race- and ranch-bred horse."*
*—Walter Merrick, on ex-pony horse Lucky 14*

THE ARRIVAL of the first Three Bars foals on the Merrick Ranch in 1953 ushered in a new era in more ways than one. Over the course of the next 14 years—through the foal crop born in 1966— the ranch's horse-breeding program would be in a state of flux.

On one hand, the Three Bars experiment had provided Walter with living proof of what the

*The Waggoner Ranch-bred Monterrey saw duty as a Merrick Ranch herd sire in the early 1950s. In addition to being credited as the sire of Easter Rose, the breedy-looking palomino sired the great Oklahoma match-racer Wilson's Yellow Cat AAA, Mission Boy AAA and AQHA Champion Monte Mischief.*

**Photo courtesy American Quarter Horse Heritage Center & Museum, Amarillo, Texas**

Thoroughbred stallion could do when crossed on his mares. Consequently, he continued to breed a few select mares to him—first in Arizona and then in California.

From that point on, he also began incorporating the blood of Three Bars into his program through a succession of top sons and grandsons—under either straight lease or shared income arrangements.

But still, the premature loss of Three Bars left Walter's program without a resident sire for an extended period of time. Just as he did before he located the stallion in Arizona, Merrick would search long and hard, and breed his mares to a variety of outside stallions before coming up with a permanent replacement.

Despite that fact, the era bounded by the early 1950s and mid-1960s was one of constant growth. Just as the Quarter Horse race and show industry was rapidly expanding in every area, so was the Merrick 14 Ranch race- and show horse program. Walter was, in fact, living out his teen-aged dream of "trying to raise some good horses."

One of the most colorful stars of this time was a mare named Easter Rose. AQHA records reveal her to be a 1953 palomino mare sired by Monterrey and out of Rose Burnett by Ben Hur II.

"I bought Easter Rose's mother off the Burnett Ranch in 1948," Walter says, "when she was a yearling. Her sire was a half-brother to Waggoner's Rainy Day P-13, and her dam was a granddaughter of Buck Thomas, the Coke Roberds-bred son of Peter McCue.

"Waggoner's Rainy Day had been known to sire a few runners. In fact, one of the better race mares in this part of the country in the late 1940s and early 1950s was a daughter of his named Raindrop. So there was some speed behind Rose Burnett on her mama's side.

"But she was almost too wild to break, so I never did try to run her. She had some buck in her that I just couldn't seem to get out. I put her in the broodmare band when she was 2, and she had a palomino filly by Revenue when she was 3. Easter Rose was her next foal."

Like her dam, Easter Rose displayed an early aversion to being ridden. She had so much potential, however, that Walter was determined to get her to the track—even if it meant the possible loss of one of his hired hands.

"In the fall of 1954," he says, "I was driving down the road one day—between Shamrock, Texas, and the ranch in Crawford—and I passed a kid on the side of the road. He was just sitting there with a little ol' tin suitcase.

"I turned around and pulled up alongside him. He looked to be about 13 years old. 'Where you headed?' I asked him. 'I don't know,' he said. 'But me and my stepdad don't get along, so I had to leave.'

"He was a little, slight-built kid, and a thought occurred to me. So I asked him, 'You ever ride any racehorses?' 'No,' he said, 'but I've ridden lots of burros.'

*The Merrick-bred Easter Rose was the 1956 AQHA Honor Roll Racehorse. Here, she wins one under the lights at Centennial. As usual Walter and Tien are present in the winner's circle shot, and Walter's irrepressible hired hand Benjamin Franklin is at the far right.*
**Photo by Ralph Morgan**

*One of the most durable runners of her era, Easter Rose went to the post an amazing 168 times—winning 33 races, finishing second 30 times and third 34 times.*

" 'Would you like to learn to ride racehorses?' I asked. 'Yes sir, I would,' he said.

"So I loaded him up in the pickup and took him home. His name was Emil Armstrong, and Tien and me got him settled in and enrolled in school. He lived with us for several years, and we raised him like he was one of our own.

"I taught that boy to ride, how to be light-handed, and how to take his bat and 'stick' a horse on the root of the tail—so they wouldn't turn sideways on him.

"He picked it up real quick, and before he got himself shot years later down in Florida, he was one of the top Quarter Horse jockeys in the nation."

The following spring, after young

Emil's arrival on the 14 Ranch, it was time to start preparing the class of '53 for the track. Among the 2-year-old prospects that year was a certain palomino mare who seemed to have the would-be jockey's number.

"Emil was a tough kid," Walter says. "He wasn't afraid of anything. But he just couldn't stay on Easter Rose. I'd put him up on her and she'd buck him off. Then we'd do it over again with the same results.

"One day, Tien and me went into town for lunch. When we came back, Emil was sittin' on the front steps of the trailer. He had his suitcase beside him and he was cryin'.

" 'What's the matter, jock?' I asked him. 'I just can't ride that damn yellow mare,' he bawled. 'She throws me off every day and I'm gettin' tired of it. I'm leaving.'

" 'Aw, calm down and go put your suitcase back in the trailer,' I said. 'You won't have to ride her anymore. I'll ride her from now on.' So I started using 'Rose' to pony the other 2-year-olds. After a while, she sorta settled down and got with the program."

Later that spring, a fellow racehorse trainer made a trip to Sayre to look over the 14 Ranch prospects.

"I was sitting on Easter Rose one day," Walter says, "when a friend of mine stopped by to look at my 2-year-olds. His name was Don Carse and he was from California.

"After he'd looked 'em all over, he said, 'Walter, you don't need all those Three Bars colts. Why don't you let me take one of them back with me to run in California?' 'I can't do that,' I said. 'They're the best prospects I've ever had and I want to keep my hands on 'em.'

" 'OK,' he said, 'If you won't let me have one of them, I'll just take that palomino mare you're riding.' I thought about it for a while, and then I just got off, pulled the saddle off, and handed her over to him. And he loaded her up and took her to the coast.

"Later that fall," Walter continues, "I was up at Centennial with my horses. We were having a great race meet with those Three Bars 2-year-

*Bob's Folly, the straightaway star of the Walter Merrick-bred crop of Three Bars foals, stood in Crawford, Oklahoma, for five years—from 1957 through 1961.*

*Among the host of top runners and show horses sired by Bob's Folly during the Crawford years was the Merrick-bred Miss Hi Jo. A 1959 bay mare out of Miss Jo Chick, Miss Hi Jo was AAA-rated on the tracks and an AQHA Champion in the show ring.*

olds. Sometimes we'd win three or four races in a day.

"Don was also there with his racing string, including Easter Rose. One day, he and Rose wound up in the same race as me and one of the Three Bars mares. My mare was named Baldy Girl II, and she was owned by Hank Wilson.

"Don came over to me and said, 'Walt, are you going to bet on this yellow mare?' 'I don't know,' I said, 'Do you think I should?' 'You damn sure better get yourself some quinellas,' he said. "A quinella bet is where you pick two horses to finish first and second, but you don't have to specify which way they finish.

"I thought about it for a little bit and then gave Tien $100 and told her to go buy 50 quinellas on Easter Rose and Baldy Girl II. Easter Rose won the race and the other mare come in second, and we won around $400."

After the Centennial race meet was over, Walter took Easter Rose back to Crawford. He continued to campaign her for four more full seasons. By the

*Walter bought Breeze Bar as a yearling in 1957. Unable to get him registered because of the roan patch of hairs visible in this photo, Walter sold the good-looking Three Bars son to Dub Phillips of Dallas, Texas. Phillips was successful in his quest to put papers on Breeze Bar and the stallion went on to be a world champion racehorse.*

**Photo by Dalco, courtesy of** *The Quarter Horse Journal*

time her career was over, the one-time bucking horse had gone to the post an amazing 168 times, winning 33 races, placing second 30 times and third 34 times. In an era of small purses, she won $43,683 and was the 1956 AQHA Honor Roll Racehorse. As if that weren't enough, she then went on to become an excellent producer.

When he wasn't running his Three Bars horses, Walter kept busy back at the ranch, trying to breed some more just like them. As previously noted, the lease of AAA-rated stallion Clovis Champ for 1954 had resulted in Clovis' Doll in 1955.

Bob's Folly's five-season stay at the ranch—from 1957 through 1961— resulted in a number of top race- and show horses. Barchick, a 1958 black mare out of Jo Chick, was a AAA runner, and Miss Hi Jo, her 1959 bay full sister, was a AAA AQHA Champion. Count Two, a 1958 chestnut stallion out of Spotted Gypsy (TB) by Spotted Bull (TB), was a AAA-rated racehorse, as was Waltz, a 1960 black mare out of Beggar Girl.

In 1957, Walter happened upon a locally-bred son of Three Bars that he immediately thought might be the permanent replacement sire he had been looking for. Unfortunately, he never got the chance to find out.

"Breeze Bar was a 1956 chestnut stallion who had been bred by J.V. Frye of Ponca City, Oklahoma," Walter said. "J.V. was a top racehorse man who had some outstanding Flying Bob-bred mares. He bred one of them, a mare named Frye's Breeze, to Three Bars the year I stood him, and then hauled another—a mare named Watch Breeze— down to Arizona two years later to breed to Three Bars. Breeze Bar was the result of the second breeding.

"When I first saw the colt as a yearling, I thought he was one of the best-looking sons of Three Bars that I'd ever seen. I bought him and even put my brand on him. I was planning on running him and then giving him a chance as a sire. Back then, half-Thoroughbreds had to be inspected before they could get papers, so I

arranged to have an AQHA inspector come out and look at him.

"Breeze Bar had a big patch of roan hair on his right side. It wasn't a spot; it didn't have pink skin under it. It was just a patch of roan hair. But the inspector turned him down because of it. I protested and hauled the colt to Amarillo to have him inspected again. They turned him down there, too."

"I wasn't about to try to build a program around a stud that couldn't be registered, so I sold him for next to nothing to Dub Phillips. He was a former rodeo champion cowboy from Dallas. Dub proceeded to have Breeze Bar inspected for the third time. They passed him.

"So I was out the money, out the horse, and then Breeze Bar went on to be exactly what I thought he would— one of the great ones. He was the 1961 AQHA Champion Quarter Running Stallion, an AQHA Champion, had an ROM in performance, and was a good sire.

"You win some, you lose some, I guess."

One of the horse deals that Walter made that turned out to be a winner involved a mare named Beggar Girl.

"Beggar Girl was a 1945 black mare by Beggar Boy (TB) and out of Baldy Girl by Oklahoma Star P-6. Hank Wilson had bred her, and he and Oscar Cox had run her. She was a top match-race mare, and, like Lena Valenti, earned a AA rating on the track back when that was the highest rating available.

"Beggar Girl was in the big package of horses I bought from Oscar in 1949. I bred her to Three Bars in 1952 and 1953 and got a couple of real nice mares as a result.

"The first was Amber's Bar, a 1953 black mare. She got hurt as a youngster, so I was never able to race her. But I kept her for a broodmare and raised a AAA runner by Blob Jr. out of her named Amber's Darling.

"Delinda, the second, was a 1954 brown mare. She did make it to the tracks and ran well enough to qualify for her AAA rating.

"Of all the mares I got from Oscar in the 1949 deal, I only kept one— Beggar Girl."

*This is Beggar Girl, a 1949 black mare by Beggar Boy (TB) and out of Baldy Girl by Oklahoma Star P-6. A winning race mare for both Hank Wilson and Oscar Cox, Beggar Girl went on to be a top producer for Walter.*

*Delinda, a 1954 black mare by Three Bars (TB) and out of Beggar Girl, was AAA-rated.*

*One of the best-looking sons of Leo, Leo Bingo was a 1955 sorrel stallion out of Beggar Girl. The Merrick-bred stallion was a AAA AQHA Champion, a top cutting horse, and a multiple AAA and AQHA Champion sire.*

*Walter acquired Miss Ruby, a top match- and pari-mutuel race mare, from Oscar Cox in 1957.*

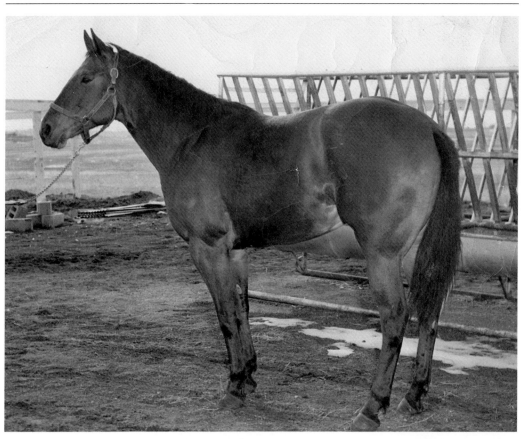

*In 1959, Miss Ruby was bred to Three Bars to produce the 1960 chestnut stallion Bar Money. Sold by Walter as a yearling for $25,000, Bar Money went on to become the second AQHA Supreme Champion and a leading sire.*
**Photo by Darol Dickinson, courtesy of** *The Quarter Horse Journal*

"Then Beggar Girl gave me a 1955 sorrel colt by Leo that I've always thought was one of the best-looking, best all-around horses I ever bred.

"I named him Leo Bingo and he was a AAA-rated racehorse, a Superior halter horse, and a top AQHA and NCHA cutting horse.

"Finally, I bred Beggar Girl to Bob's Folly four times and she had three ROM racehorses and one halter-point earner. All in all, she turned out to be one of my better early-day producers."

As was noted in the preceding chapter, Walter took two of his top mares—Lena Valenti and Miss Ruby—to the West Coast in 1960 to be bred to Three Bars. The result of the former cross was the incomparable Little Lena Bars. The result of the latter one was Bar Money.

"Of all the mares I got from Oscar in the 1949 deal," Walter says, "I only kept one—Beggar Girl. But Oscar had retained ownership of several other horses that I really wanted. One was Josie's Bar, but I never did get her. The other two were Blob Jr. and Miss Ruby. In the fall of 1957, Oscar finally let me buy those two horses and several of their offspring.

"Blob Jr. had been the 1950 AQHA Champion Quarter Running Horse, and in order to win that title he'd had to go up against the great Maddon's Bright Eyes when she was in her prime. I bred most of my mares to him in 1958, and then I sold him to the Burnett Ranch.

"Blob Jr. was a half-Thoroughbred, but he had excellent stock horse conformation and a good disposition. He was the last stallion I sold to the Burnett Ranch, and years later some of the ranch's top hands told me that he sired some of the best ranch geldings they'd ever ridden.

"I kept Miss Ruby until she died," Walter continues. "She had been a top match-race mare for Oscar, and then he'd switched her over to the pari-mutuel tracks and she'd qualified for her AAA rating. When I bred her to Three Bars, I got one of the best-looking chestnut colts ever."

By the time that colt, Bar Money, was foaled, horsemen from around the country had come to realize two things. One was that Three Bars was a pre-potent sire of not only speed, but classic Quarter Horse conformation, as well. The second thing they'd picked up on was that Walter Merrick, even though he was hid out in the red dirt hills of western Oklahoma, was raising some of the best of both kinds of horses. So, some of those horsemen began showing up in Crawford, to see what he might have for sale.

"In the spring of 1960," Walter says, "a couple of fellas named Bill Hedge and J.T. Walters showed up at my place. They were horse traders from up around Sallisaw, Oklahoma.

"They had heard about Bar Money and they came to try to buy him. After they'd looked him over, they asked me to price him. So I did—for $25,000. They left without him, but then showed back up a couple of months later.

"Before they got out to the ranch the second time, the postmaster from Crawford called me. 'Walter,' he said, 'There was a couple of fellas stopped by here a few minutes ago. They were driving a pickup and pulling a horse trailer. They didn't come in, they just unhitched their trailer and drove off. I just thought you'd wanna know.'

"Well, when those guys arrived I was ready for 'em. They started right in, trying to get me to come off my price. Finally, I said to 'em, 'Look here boys, I know you want this colt and you know you do. He's worth the dough, so why don't you just drive on back into town, hook back up to your trailer, and come and load him up?'

"Well, they had to laugh then, but that's exactly what they did. Bar Money was the highest-priced horse I'd ever sold up to that point, and he went on to be a AAA-rated racehorse, an AQHA Supreme Champion, and a good sire."

Returning to the Merrick breeding program, after Bob's Folly left for good at the conclusion of the 1961

"Bar Money was the highest-priced horse I'd ever sold up to that point."

*In 1962, Walter stood the world champion racehorse Tonto Bar Hank in Crawford for owners C. G. and Milo Whitcomb of Sterling, Colorado. After the breeding season was over, the big stallion was conditioned and taken back to the track. In this shot, he sets a new 400-yard track record in Albuquerque.*

Cooper

breeding season, the stallion that Merrick chose to replace him was once again both a top racehorse and Three Bars-bred.

"From 1962 through 1966," he says, "I stood Tonto Bars Hank for C.G. and Milo Whitcomb of Sterling, Colorado. I had gotten acquainted with them in 1950, when they came to the sale Hank Wilson and I had, and bought some mares. They were good guys and I knew I wouldn't have anything to worry about if I got into a business deal with them.

"Tonto Bars Hank was a 1958 chestnut stallion by Tonto Bars Gill by Three Bars, and out of Hanka by Hank H. by King. He didn't look like a racehorse; he stood 15-2 hands high and weighed 1,400 pounds. And he was so easy-going that Milo's young daughter, Celie, used to ride him bareback around the racetracks.

"But he was one whale of a runner.

He beat Dale Robertson's Rebel Cause in the 1960 All-American Futurity, he was the first Quarter Horse to win $100,000, and he was a three-time world champion. I stood him for the Whitcombs for the first time in 1962. We bred a full book of mares to him, and then I got him back in racing shape and took him to the track.

"He was still a pretty tough runner. In September, he won a 400-yard race at Albuquerque in :19.9. That set a track record and equaled the world and stallion records.

"Then we took him to the Centennial and Los Alamitos meets. He did well there, too, so we decided to ship him to Los Alamitos.

"He was one of the horses that got trapped in the van atop the mountain in the blizzard on the way to California—the same accident that killed Roman Bob.

" 'Hank' got sick, but he got over it

*Standing 16 hands high and weighing 1,400 pounds, Tonto Bars Hank was unusually large for a Quarter Horse sprinter. According to Walter, "In order not to get too much size and muscle mass, you had to be very careful about the kind of mare you bred to him."*

*Mine Will (TB), by I Will and out of Mined, was one of the mares that Walter chose to breed to "Hank." Hank Will (bottom), a 1966 chestnut stallion, was the resulting foal.*

*Standing 15-1 hands high and weighing 1,200 pounds, Hank Will went on to become the 20th AQHA Supreme Champion.*
**Courtesy**
*The Quarter Horse Journal*

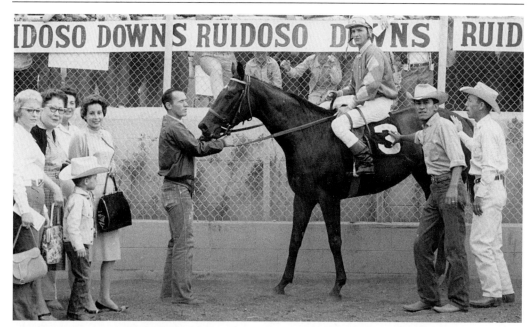

quick enough for us to run him at Los Alamitos. He wasn't the same, though—the ordeal had affected his wind—so the Whitcombs made the decision to retire him."

Merrick continued to stand Tonto Bars Hank for four more years. During that time, he also bred a number of his own mares to the ex-world champion. The results were gratifying.

Hank Will, a 1966 chestnut stallion out of Mine Will (TB), achieved a speed index of 100 and was an AQHA Supreme Champion and the 1972 AQHA High-Point Steer Roping Stallion. My Willa, a 1965 chestnut full sister to Hank Will, earned a speed index of 95.

Mr Scat Man, a 1965 chestnut stallion out of Horned Scat Bar by Bob's Folly, was an AQHA Superior Halter Horse and earned 247 open halter points. Scat Man Too, a 1966 chestnut full brother to Mr Scat Man, was an AQHA Champion.

And then there was Lucky 14, a 1964 red dun gelding by Tonto Bars Hank and out of Heart 55 by Moorehouse's Sunday.

"Lucky 14 was one of the best all-around horses I ever raised," Walter says. "He was a nice-headed, well-made colt who grew up to be a good ranch and racetrack pony horse. He had an outstanding disposition, too. Our youngest son, Joe, was born on February 7, 1957, and he pretty much learned to ride on 'Lucky.'

"I started using him as a pony horse when he was a 3-year-old, and I was still using him for one in 1969. Some folks came up to me that year and asked me to price him. I probably shouldn't have, but I did. I asked them $3,500 for him, and they gave it.

"Then they trained him and took him to the horse shows. Here he was, an unshown aged horse, and they made him a two-time AQHA Youth Champion. He also earned Superiors in open halter and Western pleasure, and two Superiors in youth Western pleasure. He wound up earning 241 halter points and 503 performance points. Not bad for a race- and ranch-bred horse."

*Mr Scat Man, a 1965 Merrick-bred chestnut stallion by Tonto Bars Hank and out of Horned Scat Bar by Bob's Folly, was an AQHA Superior Halter Horse.*

**Photo by Tom Esler, courtesy The Quarter Horse Journal**

*Lucky 14, a Merrick-bred son of Tonto Bars Hank spent years as a ranch gelding, children's mount and pony horse, before embarking on a highly successful show career. In this shot, Walter and the good-looking red dun gelding pause to allow Easy Jet a post-workout drink of water.*

In addition to standing Tonto Bars Hank in the mid-1960s, Walter also stood such horses as Missile Bar AAA by Three Bars—the 1958 AQHA Quarter Champion Running 2-Year-Old Colt and the 1959 AQHA Quarter Champion 3-Year-Old Colt; Pasamonte Paul AAA—the 1964 AQHA Quarter Champion Running Stallion; Lewin AAA by Three Bars; Red Jones (TB), AAA; Hy Diamond (TB), the maternal grandsire of All-American Futurity winner Hustling Man; and Hours Regards (TB), California 2-Year-Old Champion and stakes winner of $147,837.

All in all, the period was one marked by steady growth and the production of many of the best all-around Quarter Horses in the history of the 14 Ranch.

This was also the time during which Walter retired his two superstar sprinters—Little Lena Bars and Lena's Bar—to the broodmare band.

Unfortunately for both Merrick and the Quarter Horse breed, Little Lena Bars did not live long enough to have the chance to prove herself as a broodmare.

"Little Lena Bars had gotten injured near the end of her racing career," Walter says. "She got bumped in a race at Raton, and it messed up her hindquarters.

"We did get her bred to Tonto Bars Hank in 1966 and she had a colt named All Lit Up in 1967. He had a 96 speed index on the track and earned 10 halter points and 30 performance points.

"But before we could get her re-bred, Little Lena Bars got paralyzed in her hindquarters. She'd get down and couldn't get up, so finally we had to put her to sleep. I've always regretted losing her so early. She never had a chance to show what she was capable of producing."

On the other hand, Lena's Bar did.

Walter chose Double Bid, the 1959 AQHA Quarter Champion Running Stallion, as the sire of "Lena's" first

*The royally bred All Lit Up was a 1967 chestnut stallion by Tonto Bars Hank and out of Little Lena Bars. The only produce of his famous dam, All Lit Up was sold to Ronny Schliep of Miami, Oklahoma, and went on to become a AAA runner.*

**Photo by Quarter Racing World, courtesy *The Quarter Horse Journal***

DOUBLE DANCER

LA MESA PARK                    MAY 28,1966            W.LOVELL,UP
MY DANGER BARS (2nd)    350 yds 18:19 BANDIT'S MOLL(3rd)
W.F.MERRICK,OWNER                         PHIL GARRETT,TRAINER

*Lena's Bar, Little Lena Bar's older sister, fared better as a broodmare. Bred for the first time to Double Bid in 1962, she produced AAA-rated Double Dancer in 1963.*

foal. The resulting colt was Double Dancer, a 1963 chestnut stallion who achieved a speed index of 95.

In 1964, Walter bred Lena to Tonto Bars Hank. The result was Delta Rose, a 1964 chestnut mare. The earner of a speed index of 100, the well-conformed mare also earned three halter points.

Two years later, Lena was bred back to Tonto Bars Hank. The result this time was Mayflower Ann, a 1966 sorrel mare. Like her older full sister, she, too, achieved a speed index of 100.

Sandwiched in between the two top Tonto Bars Hank sisters was the first of two full brothers—the first of a pair of horses who not only ushered in a dramatic new era, but who redefined Walter Merrick's life.

His name was Jet Smooth.

*After Double Dancer's race career was over, Hank Wiescamp of Alamosa, Colorado, leased the stallion for several years. Utilized as an outcross stallion by the famed horse breeder in his line-bred Old Fred program, the Merrick stallion had a positive impact.*

**Photo by Darol Dickinson**

"DELTA ROSE"

LA MESA PARK, N.M.          AUG. 4, 1967          W. LOVELL, UP
ABOVE PARR 2 (2nd)         400 Yds 20.12          STREAKY JANE 2 (3rd
WALTER F. MERRICK, OWNER                          PHIL GARRETT, TRAINER

KANSAS QUARTER HORSE DERBY TRIAL WINNER

LA MESA PARK 1967

*Lena's Bar was bred to Tonto Bars Hank twice. The first cross resulted in a 1964 sorrel mare named Delta Rose. The powerfully built speedster achieved a speed index of 100 and went on to become a top producer, as well.*

*Mayflower Ann, a 1966 sorrel full sister to Delta Rose, also achieved a speed index of 100. Retired to the broodmare band, she too went on to become a top speed producer.*

# 13 A SMOOTH TRANSITION

*"I guess I wasn't meant to ever have Three Bars for long."*
*—Walter Merrick*

*The royally-bred Thoroughbred mare, Lena's Bar was a champion both on the track and in the broodmare band.*

IN 1963, Walter Merrick discovered a horse that he thought was custom-made to cross on Lena's Bar. He was a top-notch racehorse in his own right, and his pedigree came complete with a couple of Merrick all-time favorites.

"It was at the 1963 Centennial Fall race meet when I first began seriously thinking about breeding Lena's Bar to Jet Deck," he says. "He was a 4-year-old at the time and was the reigning world champion racehorse. Better yet, he was out of a daughter of Barred, Three Bars' first great Quarter Horse son. And that mare, Miss Night Barred, was out of a daughter of Midnight Jr.

"Jet Deck was about the hottest thing going as far as the Centennial crowd was concerned. The more he ran, the more he seemed to just run off and hide from the competition. People were starting to talk like he couldn't be beat. And I could see he was good. But I thought I had something at home that could give him a run for his money.

"Toward the end of the meet, I sidled up to Leo Winters, a friend of mine from Durant, Oklahoma, and said, 'They're pretty high on that colt, aren't they?' 'They sure are,' he said.

" 'Here's what I want you to do,' I told him. 'Circulate around and see if you can scare up a match race between Jet Deck and Lena's Bar.' I'd retired 'Lena,' but she was young and sound and I didn't think it would take long to whip her into shape.

" 'How far do you want to run and how much do you want to run for?' Leo asked. 'The distance doesn't matter,' I said, 'but I wouldn't want to go to all the trouble of getting my mare ready for less than $10,000.'

"So, Leo moseyed around and tried to make a match. A couple of days later, he came back and reported that it was a 'no go.'

" 'Walter,' he said, 'I can't believe it. Jet Deck is about the toughest racehorse running today, and he's quick away from the gate. But I'll tell you what. I've talked to Jay Chambers, his owner, and to Wilbur Stuchal, his trainer, and they just don't want any part of your little Thoroughbred mare—at any distance.' "

*Jet Deck, the sire of Lena's Bar's first foal, was a five-time world champion racehorse who earned $200,628 on the straightaways. On the bottom side of his pedigree, he traced back to both Three Bars and Midnight Jr. He is shown here being exercised by jockey Charles Smith.*

**Courtesy of The Quarter Horse Journal**

"But I still liked Jet Deck," Walter continues. "I figured, if I can't match Lena's Bar against him one way, I might as well do it another way. So I bred her to him."

As it turned out, Jet Deck was retired from racing at the end of the 1964 season. Bud Warren—of Leo and Sugar Bars fame—arranged to stand the world champion in Perry, Oklahoma.

Lena's Bar would be the first mare bred to him.

"I hauled Lena to Bud's place in the spring of 1964," Walter says. "I arrived there in the late afternoon. The mare was in heat, so Bud and I bred her to Jet Deck. I stayed overnight at Bud's, and the next morning we bred the two again. Then I loaded her up and took her home. And Jet Smooth was born at Crawford the following spring.

"There's been some rumors," he continues, "that Jet Smooth was not sired by Jet Deck. The gossips said he was too good-looking to be a Jet Deck,

that he had to be by Sugar Bars.

"All I can say to that is, I was there when the mare was bred. And she was bred to Jet Deck. That's all there is to it."

Jet Smooth was indeed a fine-looking individual. A dark chestnut in color, he sported a strip face and four white socks. Although Walter had never been enamored with halter competition, he did turn the race-bred youngster over to Jerry Wells of Sulphur, Oklahoma, to show at one show as a yearling.

The occasion was the Tri-State Fair, held in September in Amarillo, Texas. Entered in the Golden Spread yearling stallion halter futurity, Jet Smooth placed first. Entered in the open halter competition, in a class of 14, he placed first again.

After the show, he was returned to Walter's care to begin training for the career for which he had been bred.

The arrival of Jet Smooth on the scene signaled the beginning of a new

*The resulting foal from the Jet Deck – Lena's Bar mating, Jet Smooth was a 1965 chestnut colt with a diamond marking on his forehead and white on all four legs.*

era for Walter Merrick and the 14 Ranch. The stallion was by far the best-looking, best-bred, most exciting young race prospect that the ranch had produced in the last decade.

But, as good as he was, and as excited as Walter was about what the future held in store for him, Jet Smooth was not the only sign that the times were changing.

By the fall of 1966, Walter could see that his horse operation had drastically outgrown his Crawford facility. There simply weren't enough barns, runs or corrals to accommodate the growing number of outside mares being transported in to be bred to the ranch's race sires.

On top of that, the ranch was situated in too remote a location. Walter felt he needed to re-locate to a place that was more accessible to the public. So he initiated a serious search for a new home.

Late in the year, he settled on an expansive race plant located on the

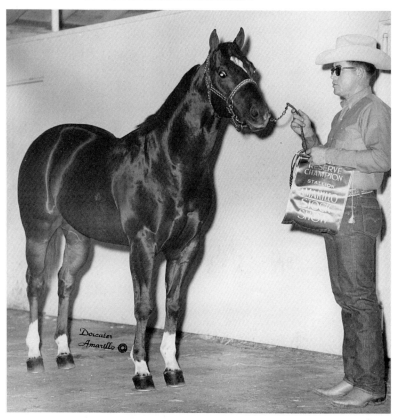

*Shown by Jerry Wells as a yearling, Jet Smooth won the yearling class at the 1966 Tri-State Fair in Amarillo, Texas.*
**Photo by Dalco**

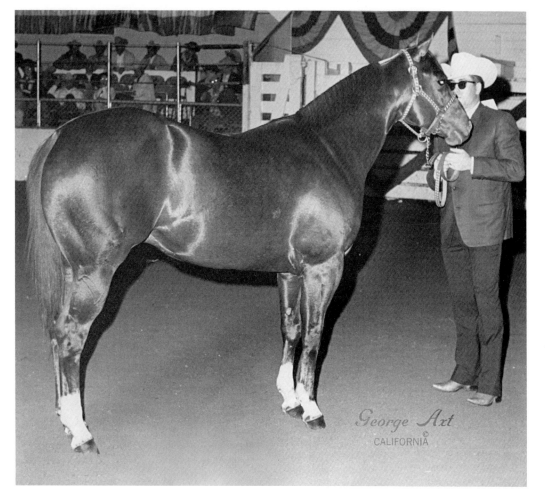

*This is Jet Smooth the halter horse as a 3-year-old. Exhibited by Jerry Wells at the 1968 Southwestern Livestock Exposition and Fat Stock Show in Fort Worth, the well-made stallion placed second in a class of 22.*
**Photo by George Axt**

outskirts of Quannah, Texas. The facility was a rambling affair, with stud barns and runs, a mare motel and breeding shed, and broodmare and yearling paddocks—all enclosed within miles of pipe fencing.

Still, Walter was not sure he was completely satisfied with the ranch, so he arranged to lease it for one breeding season, with an option to buy. He moved his family and his horses down to their new home and got them all settled in.

"At the time I moved down to Quannah," Walter says, "I had three or four nice studs to stand. I had Missile Bar and Lewin, and I also had a new Thoroughbred stud that I was pretty high on. His name was Good Bird, and he was a 1956 chestnut stallion sired by Papa Redbird and out of Goody by Menow.

"Good Bird hadn't been bred to very many Quarter mares when I got him, but Bird Man, one of his Thoroughbred colts, had competed on the Quarter tracks and run top AAA. But I thought I needed another good Quarter Horse stud to stand, so I flew out to California in December to see if I could find one.

"They were having a big racehorse sale at Pomona, California, and I had planned it to be my first stop. The sale got underway, and then it got to be lunchtime. I was standing in line waiting to get something to eat when I noticed Sid Vail and his wife, Mayola, sitting in a booth, looking at me and talking. Finally, Sid got up and came over to where I was.

" 'Walt,' he said, 'after you get your food, come on over to the booth. Mayola and I want to talk to you a

*In 1967, Walter Merrick and Three Bars were re-united and, that year, the stallion stood to a full book of mares at Quannah, Texas. Even at the age of 27, the stallion was still the epitome of refinement and class.*

**Photo by Darol Dickinson, courtesy Jim Senkbeil**

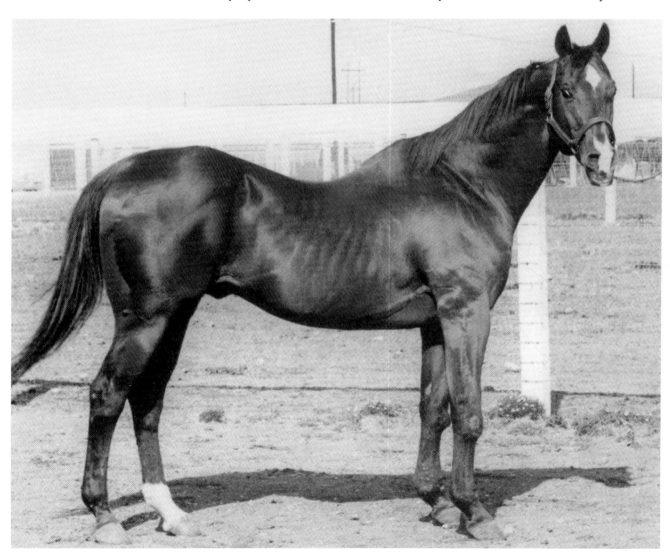

little bit.' So I went over there. Mayola had been crying and she said, 'Walter, you took a chance on Three Bars before anyone knew him and he never looked better than when you had him. We were just wondering if you'd be interested in taking him back.'

" 'What kind of condition is he in?' I asked. 'Is he still breeding mares?' 'He's in great shape,' Sid said. 'He'd breed a mare a day if you'd want him to.'

"Sid's vet, Dr. Becker, was at the sale, so I hunted him up to ask his opinion about Three Bars' breeding shape. He said the horse was strong, so I went back over to Sid and Mayola.

"Sid had been standing Three Bars for $10,000. I said to him, 'I don't think I can stand him in Texas for $10,000. But I do think I can get $5,000. And we'll split it right down the middle. 'OK,' Sid said. "Come and get him. But there is one stipulation. He's taken up with an old blind mare named Fairy Adams. You've got to take her, too.' 'That's all right,' I said."

Upon returning to Texas, Walter immediately hooked his pickup truck to a two-horse trailer, got his assistant farm manager, Johnny T.L. Jones, to go with him, and headed back to the coast to pick up Three Bars.

"After I got them back to Quannah," Walter says, "I kept Three Bars and Fairy Adams in adjoining stalls in the stud barn. Even that wasn't enough, though. I had to knock out some boards so that he could see her.

"In 1967, I bred him to a full book of mares. He was in good shape for his age, and Tien and me would take turns getting him out during the day and letting him graze for an hour or so on the lawn or on the wheat pasture. Sometimes we'd have to take the old mare with. He'd graze a lot better if he could see her.

"By the end of the 1967 breeding season," he continues, "I could see that the Quannah Ranch was not going to work out. It was just too spread out. It was hard to get around and get things done. So I bought 1,600 acres just south of Sayre and started building a home and horse breeding facility from the ground up.

"By the time the breeding season started in February, the place was mostly complete and I'd moved my family and the horses onto it. And we had another good book of mares lined up to breed to Three Bars and Good Bird.

"One day near the end of March, before the season had really even gotten started, I was outside helping some guys build a pipe fence. One of the barn helpers came running up to me and said, 'You better come up and look at Three Bars; something's wrong with him.'

"I ran up and went into his stall. He was standing there panting, and he had his nostrils flared out like he'd been running. I thought he was having a heart attack, so I called Dr. Fred Rule, my vet, and told him to come out.

"Fred arrived and put a stethoscope to Three Bars' chest. 'His heart is just flying,' he said. 'It sounds like a washing machine.' Well, there wasn't much we could do. We stayed with him until about 3 o'clock the next morning, and then he died.

"I called Sid and gave him the bad news," he continues. "He had moved to a ranch near Nocona, Texas, by this time. I asked him what he wanted me to do with Three Bars, and he said to bring the horse down to him so he could bury him.

*In this head and shoulder study of Three Bars and one of his most loyal fans, the stallion's damaged right nostril is apparent. He suffered the injury in 1952 at Walter's Crawford Ranch.*

**Photo by Darol Dickinson, courtesy Jim Senkbeil**

"I wanted to bury him here, but it wasn't my call. It was hard for me to load him up and haul him off. To make matters worse, Sid didn't even stay on the Nocona place long. He pulled up stakes and went back to California.

"I guess I wasn't meant to ever have Three Bars for long. But, as it turns out, I had him long enough. And he sure was good to me and my family."

From Three Bars' last full foal crop, born in 1968, would come a number of top performers.

No Double, a Merrick-bred sorrel stallion out of Miss Bound Away by Chick Away, achieved a speed index of 95 and was an AQHA Champion with 35 halter and 11 performance points. Carlotta 2, a bay mare out of Twayna by Rebel Cause, achieved a 97 speed index and won the Sunland Spring Futurity and $67,685.

Jet Along, a black stallion out of Waltz, achieved a 90 speed index, and

*No Double, a Merrick-bred 1968 chestnut stallion by Three Bars and out of Miss Bound Away, achieved a speed index of 95 and earned an AQHA Championship with 35 halter and 11 performance points.*

Ontila Zeua, a sorrel stallion out of Rita Girl by Joe Reed II, had a 93 speed index.

Mr Go Bar, Tet Bare, Three Bars Queen, Three Dreams and Top Sargeant all achieved 90 or higher speed indexes.

From the legendary stallion's last foal crop, born in 1969 and numbering seven, came only one Register of Merit performer. The Last Son, a bay stallion out of Fairy Adams, earned 11 points and an ROM in performance. His dam—Three Bars' faithful companion—would pass away two years later, at the age of 22.

Once and for all time, Three Bars was gone. But Walter had a grandson of his to replace him, who was as good-looking as they come and who was tearing them up on the straightaway tracks.

"In addition to helping me run the ranch," Walter says, "Johnny Jones was a racehorse trainer. In 1967, I sent

*Waltz, a 1960 black mare by Bob's Folly and out of Beggar Girl, achieved a AAA track rating. Retired to the broodmare band, she went on to produce four runners with speed indexes of 90 or higher.*

*Jet Along, a Merrick-bred 1968 black stallion by Three Bars and out of Waltz by Bob's Folly, also achieved a 90 speed index.*

*The same year Three Bars was returned to Walter Merrick's care, the stallion's grandson Jet Smooth won the Kansas Futurity at Ruidoso Downs in Ruidoso, New Mexico.*

*In 1968, Jet Smooth won the All-American Congress Futurity in Ohio. Pictured with the flashy stallion in this winner's circle shot are, from left, Jim and Walter Merrick, and trainer John T. L. Jones.*

him and Jet Smooth to Ruidoso to get ready to run. Johnny got along real well with the colt, and in August, Jet Smooth won the Kansas Futurity at Ruidoso.

"We had him entered in the All-American Futurity on Labor Day, and going into the time trials he was the favorite to win it all. Then, right before his heat, Johnny had his groom bring Jet Smooth to the saddling paddock.

"The colt was feeling frisky and he got away from the groom and went roaring around the race grounds. It took us a while to get him corralled, and by that time he'd run his race. He didn't even make the finals."

Once he got over his initial disappointment of not doing well in the All-American, Walter continued campaigning Jet Smooth—at both halter and racing.

The highlight of Jet Smooth's sophomore campaign was his victory in the 440-yard World's Championship Classic at Ruidoso Downs.

Jet Smooth's daughter Smooth Pebble achieved a speed index of 90 and produced seven runners with speed indexes of 90 or higher.

*In this priceless photo taken in 1967 in Quannah, Texas, Walter takes Three Bars out for his daily lawn-grazing break. The great sire passed away the following year at Walter's new ranch south of Sayre, Oklahoma.*

**Photo by Darol Dickinson, courtesy Jim Senkbeil**

After the Labor Day race, the 2-year-old was returned to Jerry Wells to fit for the show ring. From September through November of 1967, the pair competed in 10 shows, winning two grands, three reserves, eight firsts and two seconds. The two second-place ribbons were earned in the toughest competition of the day—in a class of 22 at the Chicago International in November 1967, and in a class of 22 at the Southwestern Livestock Exposition and Fat Stock Show in Fort Worth in February 1968.

In the spring of his 3-year-old year, still under the guidance of Johnny Jones, Jet Smooth was returned to the track. Mid-way through the season, he placed third in the New Mexico State Fair Handicap at Albuquerque. In October, he won the All-American Congress Derby at Beulah Park in Columbus, Ohio—setting a 400-yard track record in the process.

While in Columbus, Jet Smooth was also entered in the halter competition at the All-American Quarter Horse Congress, and, in racing shape, placed second in a class of 15 three-year-old stallions.

Back on the track for his final year of campaigning as a 4-year-old, the durable stallion won the World's Championship Classic and placed third in the Three Bars Handicap at Ruidoso. He also ran third in the C. L. Maddon Bright Eyes Handicap at Albuquerque.

In 1971, Jet Smooth made one last trip to the halter ring. On April 16, in Elk City, Oklahoma, he earned Grand Champion Stallion and First Place Aged Stallion honors.

Understandably so, Walter was proud of his double-Three Bars-bred champion. And he was eager to see what Jet Smooth could accomplish in the breeding shed.

"There's never been a doubt in my mind about how good Jet Smooth was," Walter says. "At the time he hit the ground, he was far and away the best colt I'd ever bred. He was good-looking enough to stand with the best halter horses in the nation, and he was fast enough to hang with the faster racehorses of his day.

"As a breeding horse, he went on to sire world champion runners like Smooth Coin, and big-time cutting horses like Smooth Herman. And he sired halter horses, pleasure horses and rope horses, as well.

"All in all, I thought Jet Smooth was everything a Quarter Horse should be. In fact, there was only one thing that kept him from being one of the all-time great horses of the breed.

"As great as he'd been as a show horse and racehorse, Jet Smooth never got the chance to prove what he could do as a sire.

"It wasn't intentional on my part. I never quit believing in him.

"But racehorses were still my first love, and two years after I bred Jet Smooth, I bred a full brother to him who was the fastest thing that I'd ever been connected with.

"I called him Easy Jet."

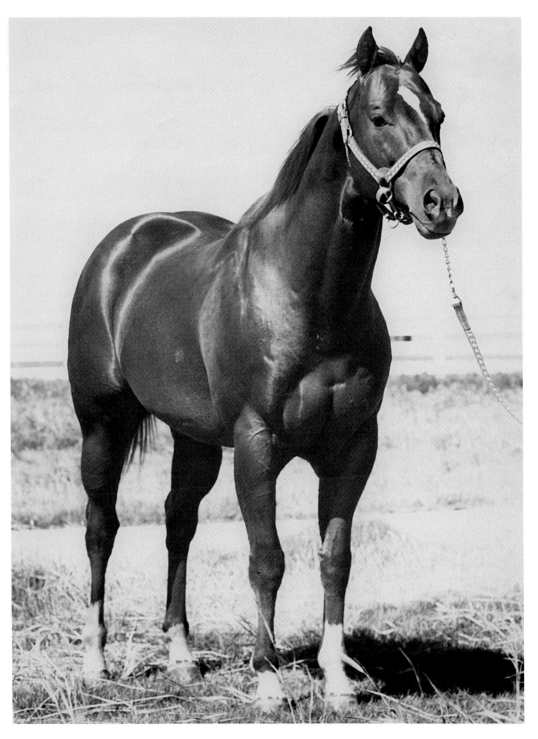

*A world-class runner and halter horse, Jet Smooth went on to sire race earners of more than $2.5 million.*
**Photo by Darol Dickinson**

# 14 EASY STREET

*"When the hot blood of Three Bars hit the blood of ol' Midnight,
the speed, it came easy, and Jet was his name.
Well, the rest is all history, and for some it's a mystery,
but America's horses were never the same."*
—Joe Merrick, from Ranches & Rodeos
*(c) 1997 BMI*

**"He was a bundle of energy from the day he was born."**

NOT LONG after Three Bars re-entered Walter Merrick's life for the last time, a Quarter Horse colt who would become the legendary stallion's most accomplished heir entered it for the first.

"After Jet Smooth was foaled in 1965," Walter says, "I gave a lot of thought to hauling Lena's Bar right back to Jet Deck. I decided against it, though, for one reason. I didn't want anything to happen to the colt. I didn't want him out of my sight.

"So I bred 'Lena' to Tonto Bars Hank, who was standing at my place that year. Mayflower Ann was the result."

In 1966, with Jet Smooth maturing into a beautiful, well-balanced halter and race prospect, Walter couldn't stand it anymore. He hauled Lena's Bar back to Perry, Oklahoma, to be bred to Jet Deck for the second and last time. Easy Jet, the resulting foal, was born in Quannah, Texas, on January 12, 1967.

The chestnut colt would be his famous dam's last offspring. Shortly after he was weaned, Lena's Bar died of a bladder infection.

"Easy Jet was not ever as pretty as Jet Smooth," Walter says. "But he had a way of making you look at him anyway. He was a big, rugged colt, with good bone and very correct in the legs.

"And he was a bundle of energy from the day he was born. He was always busy. When he was a yearling, I kept him in a paddock with five or six other colts the same age. Easy Jet like to wore them out.

"He'd run up to them, rear and nip at one or another, and get the whole bunch riled up and moving. Then he'd take off and leave 'em in the dust. Then he'd maybe stop and look around a bit. But pretty soon, here he'd come again, ready to start the whole ruckus all over again. I'm not sure when he ate. He must of some at night, because he always kept his weight up and he grew fast.

"And Easy Jet was a handful when it came time to leg him up as long yearling," Walter continues. "A fella who worked for me named Benjamin Franklin was the one who first started ponying him.

"Benjamin was a black man from Louisiana who Oscar Cox had employed back when he was running Blob Jr. and Josie's Bar. When Oscar sold out in 1950, Benjamin came to work for me. He was a character—always quick to grin and joke around—and he was with me for more than 19 years.

Benjamin was also a top hand with horses, so I turned to him when it got time to start legging Easy Jet up.

*Easy Jet—world champion racehorse and founder of one of the most accomplished speed lines in the history of the Quarter Horse breed.*

**Photo by Orren Mixer**

Things proceeded according to plan for awhile. Then, one day Benjamin came up to me and said, 'Mr. Walt, I hate to have to say this, but I just can't pony that colt no more.' 'Why not?' I asked. 'Cause he's got to the point where he thinks he should be sittin' in the saddle with me.'

"When it came time to break 'Jet' to ride, he was the same kind of handful. Not that he was mean or prone to buck. He was just so quick that sometimes he'd dump his rider just goofing around. But we eventually got him to where he pointed straight ahead most of the time, and I could see he had some speed."

Just as he had with Mona Leta 15 years earlier, Walter opted to start Easy Jet for the first time in late December of his yearling year. The occasion was an unofficial yearling race at Sallisaw, Oklahoma, and with jockey Elbert Minchey up, the result was an easy, four-length win.

The sneak-preview event afforded the Quarter racing community its first glimpse at Merrick's promising young prospect, and that look resulted in the first legitimate offer to buy him.

"After Easy Jet won that yearling race so handily," Walter says, "a well-known Quarter race trainer, who went on to become one of the all-time leading Thoroughbred trainers, offered me $75,000 for Jet. But I realized by this time that I had my hands on something really special, so I turned it down."

Two weeks later, in early January, Easy Jet went to the post for the first time as a 2-year-old in the trials of the 330-yard, $61,486 Blue Ribbon Downs Futurity, also held at Sallisaw. It was the beginning of a freshman campaign that would go down in Quarter racing lore as one of the most legendary ever.

As he had in the yearling race, Walter tapped Minchey as Jet's jockey for the Blue Ribbon trials and finals. The results were official victories numbers one and two.

Two months later, the scene shifted to Columbus, Texas, for the 300-yard, $53,166 Columbus Triple Crown

Futurity. With Minchey still in the irons, Jet breezed to victory number three in the trials on March 9 and victory number four in the finals on March 23.

One week later, the Merrick-Jet-Minchey team were at the newly constructed La Bahia Downs in Goliad, Texas, for the trials and finals of the 330-yard, $24,069 Texas Futurity. After winning his trial heat on March 30, Easy Jet suffered his first defeat of the year—finishing second to Mighty Moon in the finals.

In May, the location shifted to Lubbock Downs, with the results being first-place finishes in the trials and futurity finals and a race record that now stood at six starts, five wins, one second.

Next up was the biggest prize to date—the 350-yard, $136,595 Kansas Futurity, to be run in the pines at New Mexico's Ruidoso Downs. The result was two more victories, including an impressive 1½-length win over Miss Three Wars and Black Mood in the June 15th finals.

On June 27, still at Ruidoso, Jet went to the post for the ninth time in the trials of the prestigious 330-yard Oklahoma Futurity. It was at this juncture that Minchey chose to withdraw as the sprinter's regular jockey.

"Elbert was an outstanding rider," Walter says, "but he had a tendency to drink a little and stay out late partying on the night before a race. Still, we won our trial heat for the Oklahoma Futurity and were set to come back in the finals on July 6. Elbert showed up the day of the race a little worse for the wear. He wasn't as sharp as he should've been, and we lost the race by a length to Hell's To Betsy.

"Afterwards, I pulled Elbert aside and had a little talk with him about his carousing. He decided it was time to call it quits. I owed him $25,000 in mount and purse money, and I paid him off. He went straight into town and put it as a down-payment on a bar."

Easy Jet's next scheduled contest was less than three weeks away.

"Running came so easy to him, he'd have a tendency to not take it very seriously. It was fun to him. "

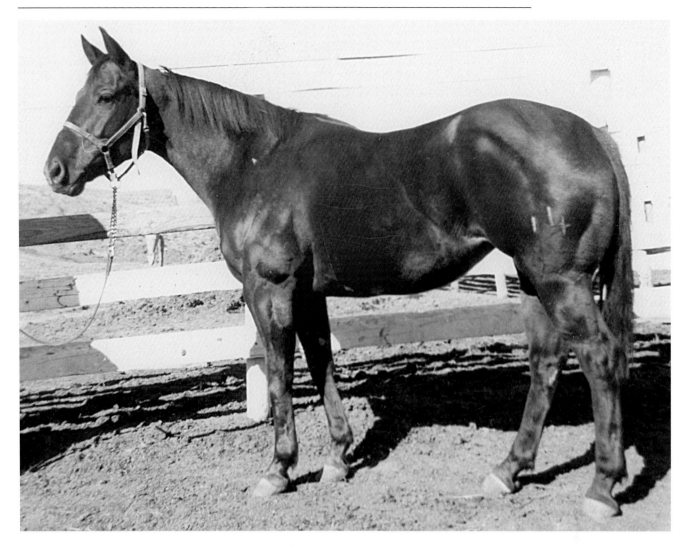

*Here is Lena's Bar, Easy Jet's AAA-rated Thoroughbred dam, at home on the Crawford Ranch in 1960.*

Entered in the trials of the 400-yard Raton Futurity at La Mesa Park in Raton, New Mexico, the strapping 2-year-old colt placed first with jockey Ray Spencer in the irons.

Merrick then promptly loaded Jet up and hauled him back to Ruidoso to compete in the August 1 trials of the Rainbow Futurity. Willie Lovell got the mount for this race, and he piloted Jet to a win.

Then it was back on the road again to Raton. In the Raton Futurity finals on August 3, with Spencer once more aboard, Easy Jet ran second to Three Deep.

Two days later, Merrick and his charge were back in Ruidoso for the Rainbow finals. It was at this point that the double-bred Three Bars colt, with Lovell aboard, suffered his worst outing of the season.

"If Easy Jet had a weakness at all,"

Walter says, "it was that running came so easy to him, he'd have a tendency to not take it very seriously. It was fun to him.

"Sometimes, he'd stand in the starting gate with a hind leg cocked, just sort of gawking around. In the Rainbow finals, he wasn't standing right. He had one hind foot behind the breaking bar, so one of the gate men went up and kicked him on the foot to make him move it.

"Easy Jet must have thought the race was off. He hit the closed head gate so hard he knocked a couple of teeth out. It addled him and he set back on the tailgate. The starter opened the gates an instant later and the horses broke out. Jet got away bad, so Willie didn't even push him. He just breezed him to a fifth-place finish. But he still covered the distance in AAA time."

Mid-way through the racing season, Easy Jet's record stood at 16 starts, 12 wins, three seconds and one fifth. Up next was a shot at the biggest prize of all—the All-American Futurity. Lovell was now Jet's regular rider, and would be the only jockey to pilot him from this point on.

As it is today, the 1969 All-American Futurity was the crown jewel of Quarter Horse racing. Conceived in the late 1950s by then-Ruidoso Downs owner Gene Hensley and a handful of Quarter racehorse men, the race was first run on September 7, 1959. The gross purse was an unheard-of $129,686. Winner of the inaugural 400-yard event was Galobar, a 1957 sorrel mare by Three

Bars (TB) and out of Josephine R.—and thus a full sister to Oscar Cox's renown Josie's Bar.

By the time the race's 11th edition was scheduled to be run on September 1, 1969, the gross purse had grown to $400,140, and the event was rightfully billed as "the world's richest horse race."

Despite his setbacks in the recent Raton and Rainbow futurities, Easy Jet was the odds-on favorite to claim the big Labor Day prize. On August 22, with Lovell in the irons, he lived up to his advance billing, winning his trial heat over Go Mobile and Pal's Peggy Bird in the excellent time of :20.10.

The track condition for the finals was a factor. Officially listed as sloppy,

*Easy Jet's first stakes victory, with jockey Elbert Minchey aboard, came in the January 12, 1969, finals of the Blue Ribbon Futurity at Sallisaw, Oklahoma.*

"Easy Jet"  E.MINCHEY UP  300 YDS.
COLUMBUS TRIPLE CROWN FUTURITY 1ST DIVISION-PURSE $103,000.00
OWNER & TRAINER: WALTER MERRICK
2ND. CUTER YET-3RD. FLAMING SQUAW-4TH. HOWDY JONES
COLUMBUS, TEXAS 3/23/69

COLUMBUS RACE COURSE

COLUMBUS TRIPLE CROWN FUTURITY
WINNER 1ST DIVISION
1969

courtesy of a recent rainstorm the track was actually a sea of mud.

For a horse the caliber of Easy Jet, however, the surface didn't matter all that much. Breaking on top from the number two post position, he grabbed the early lead and held off all challengers to win by a neck over Miss Three Wars, with Velox Bar finishing third, one length back. The winning time over the slow track was :20.46 and the winner's share of the purse was $159,840.

Easy Jet had arrived.

By this time, the Merrick-bred superstar had been christened with the nickname "Calhoun." The moniker came, according to Walter, courtesy of Benjamin Franklin.

"Benjamin used to tell a story," he says, "about a high school football player from down in Louisiana named Calhoun.

"Calhoun was a running back, and, according to Benjamin, he could always be counted on to get that extra yard on the ground. During one particularly tough game, all the coach would holler in from the sideline was, 'Give Calhoun the ball! Give Calhoun the ball!'

"Finally, Calhoun had enough. Before the next play, the coach hollered in to the quarterback, 'Give Calhoun the ball!' After a brief pause, the quarterback raised his head up out of the huddle and said, 'Coach . . . Calhoun don't want the ball!'

"We were running Easy Jet so often that Benjamin started calling him Calhoun. And the name just kind of stuck."

*The Blue Ribbon crown was followed by a victory in the Columbus Triple Crown Futurity at Columbus, Texas.*

159

"THE KANSAS QUARTER HORSE FUTURITY"
PURSE $136,595.20    HORSE EASY JET
OWNER WALTER MERRICK    DISTANCE 350 YARDS    2ND MISS THREE WARS
TRAINER OWNER    TIME :17.60    DATE 6-15-69    3RD BLACK MOOD
JOCKEY E. MINCHEY    RUIDOSO DOWNS, RUIDOSO DOWNS, N. M.    BY TIL THOMPSON

*On June 15, 1969, Easy Jet raced to an impressive 1½-length victory in the $136,595 Kansas Futurity at Ruidoso Downs in Ruidoso, New Mexico. The win photo illustrates how the powerful sprinter usually ran with his ears flicking back and forth.*

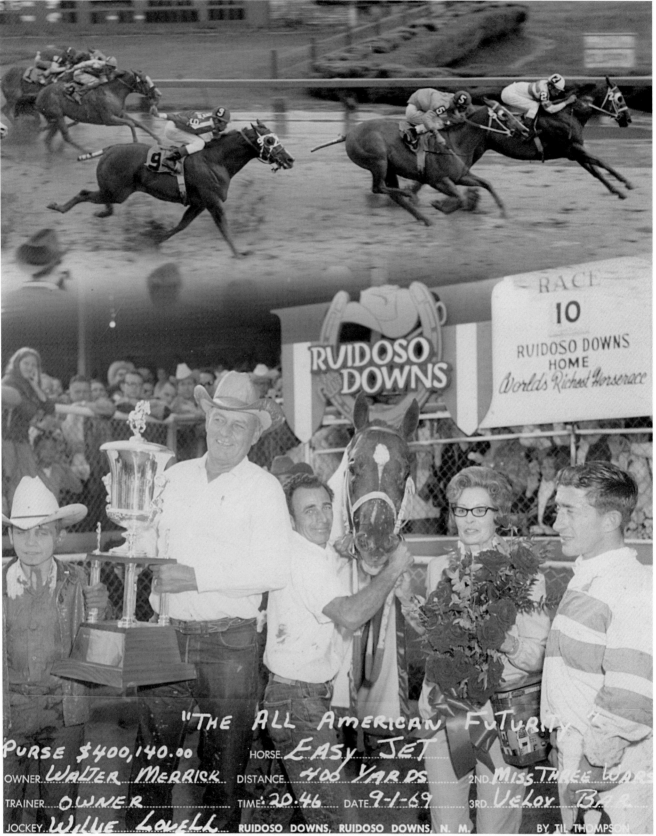

The dream of a lifetime comes true as Easy Jet, with Willie Lovell aboard, splashes to a half-length victory over Miss Three Wars in the 1969 All-American Futurity at Ruidoso Downs. In the exciting moments leading up to post time, 12-year-old Joe Merrick told his mother that if "Jet" won the big one, he was going to dive headfirst onto the muddy track. Distracted, Tien replied, "That will be fine." The picture tells the rest of the story.

*Mile-high Centennial Race Track, located on the southern outskirts of Denver, proved to be one of Easy Jet's favorite tracks. In the fall of 1969, he notched victories in both the Colorado Laddie Stakes and the Rocky Mountain Quarter Horse Association Futurity.*

**Photos by Ralph Morgan**

After the All-American, it would be more than three weeks before Merrick would hand the ball back to Calhoun. And then it would be in the mile-high atmosphere of Denver, Colorado.

On September 24, Easy Jet won his trial heat of the 400-yard, $18,825 Colorado Laddie Stakes, held at Centennial Race Track in Denver. Four days later, he won the finals by 4½ lengths over Charlie Hall and Red Man Chick. One month later, still at Centennial, he and Lovell notched another win in the trial heat of the 400-yard, $40,373 RMQHA Futurity. In the finals on October 22, the duo breezed to a one-length victory over Jaguar's Go Go and Carter Decker.

It was then "head east" time for the Merrick-bred flying machine. The target this time was Beulah Park in Columbus, Ohio—the home of the 350-yard, $34,300 All-American Congress Futurity.

With more than 1,200 miles separating the two tracks, Walter decided that maybe he should give his 2-year-old charge a mid-trip rest break.

"Easy Jet was always a handful," he says, "even when he was being run steady. Around half-way between Denver and Columbus, I decided I needed to get him out of the trailer and let him rest and walk around a bit.

"So we pulled over and I unloaded him. After about five minutes I said to the boys who were traveling with me, 'Let's load him back up and hit the road. If we don't, I'm afraid he's gonna get loose on me and start running down the blacktop.'

"Even after all he'd been through, he was still a handful to handle."

Handful or not, Easy Jet managed to get enough rest on the cross-country journey to go to the post in the Columbus futurity and win both his trial heat on November 1 and the finals two days later.

Only one obstacle remained for the

*At the All-American Congress Futurity in Columbus, Ohio, Easy Jet raced to a two-length victory in the mud. In the winner's circle photo, from left, are Walter, Blair Folck, Tien, Bob Willoughby and jockey Willie Lovell.*

Throughout his record-setting 26-race freshman campaign, Easy Jet was afforded the best care possible. Here, Walter and Willie Lovell rinse the young stallion down after a workout.

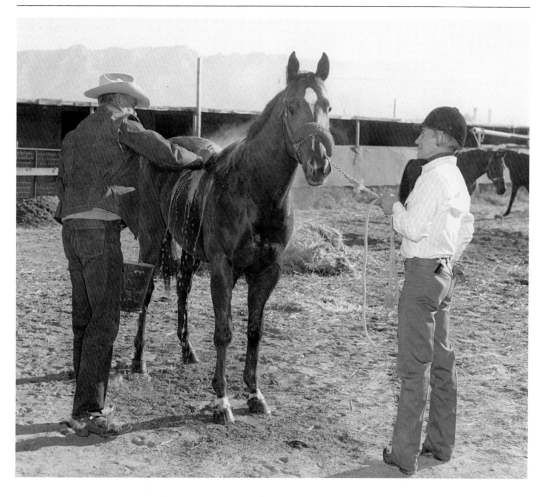

Walter credits daily water turbulation treatments with having a positive impact on his efforts to keep Easy Jet sound and free from soreness. Here, "Jet" is not sure what he thinks of the procedure.

durable freshman sprinter that year. That was the 400-yard, $52,800 Sunland Fall Futurity in El Paso, Texas. On November 21, with Lovell up, Easy Jet won his trial heat. On November 30, he duplicated that effort, winning the finals by two lengths over Our Mott and Jet Deep.

Easy Jet's 2-year-old campaign had now drawn to an end, and what a glorious battle it had been: 26 starts, 22 wins, three seconds and one fifth. Nine stakes wins, with four of them—the All-American, the All-American Congress, the Triple Crown and the Sunland Fall futurities—run in the mud. A fifth, the RMQHA Futurity was run in rain and snow.

Easy Jet's earnings for the year—$409,155—established a new single-year record, and he was named the 1979 World Champion, 1979 World Champion Stallion and 1979 World Champion Two-Year-Old Colt.

For all connected with it, the year and the campaign was one to be forever remembered and cherished. It was also one that was the subject of a certain amount of criticism.

"Some people got on me pretty hard about how often I ran Easy Jet," Walter says. "They said I was too hard on him, that I didn't care about him and that I was going to ruin him. I didn't pay too much attention to them. I knew my horse.

"Easy Jet was not an easy horse to be around. And it didn't matter whether you were walking him, or galloping him, or racing him—it was the same. He had a seemingly endless supply of drive and energy. If I hadn't run him so much, I'd still have had to work the living daylights out of him. And if I was going to have to do that, I just reckoned it made more sense to put him in a race.

"As far as not caring about him and not taking care of him, I'll never know where that came from.

"He was the only horse I had in training that year. Between myself; Bob Willoughby, Curtis' and Ruby's son; my son Joe; and Benjamin Franklin, we lived with that horse seven days a week, 24 hours a day.

Joe, who was 12 at the time, used to sleep on a cot in front of Jet's stall.

"And I used to turbulate his legs a lot. I'd spend an hour a day doing that. It kept him from getting sore. But even that caused some rumors. People would say, 'We won't have to worry about Easy Jet no more; he's broke down.'

"I don't know of any other horse who ever had the kind of 2-year-old year that Easy Jet had," Walter continues. "Twenty-seven starts, counting the yearling race, with 23 wins and three seconds.

"The horse was born to run. He loved it. A lot of racehorses run scared; they run with their ears pinned back. Easy Jet usually ran with his working forward and back. He was just playing most of the time.

"And he never took a sore step that entire season. I know. I was with him every inch of the way."

As was to be expected, after his freshman campaign, interest in breeding to Easy Jet was at a fever pitch. He was returned to Walter's new Sayre, Oklahoma, 14 Ranch racing and breeding plant and advertised at stud, with his fee set at $2,000.

After standing to a full book of mares in the late winter of 1969 and early spring of 1970, the now-3-year-old racehorse was returned to the track.

Easy Jet's first start as a sophomore runner came in late June, in the Rainbow Derby trials at Ruidoso Downs. He placed third, but still qualified for the finals. In that event, on July 5, the reigning world champion runner placed dead last for the first and only time in his racing career. Walter was quick to place the blame for the stallion's dismal performance squarely on his own shoulders.

"After his long 2-year-old campaign and then a heavy breeding season, I probably rushed Easy Jet back into competition," he says. "I should have taken it slower with him. I wanted him in the Rainbow Derby but he just wasn't ready for it. After it, I backed

"After his long 2-year-old campaign and then a heavy breeding season, I probably rushed Easy Jet back into competition."

"EASY JET"
"THE RATON QUARTER HORSE DERBY—$25,250.00"
LA MESA PARK, N.M.        SEPT. 13, 1970        W. LOVELL, UP
RELLER (2nd)                400 Yds 19.69        GO TOGETHER (3rd)
WALTER F. MERRICK, OWNER & TRAINER

*After taking most of the summer to round back into top form, Easy Jet scored his first big sophomore win in the finals of the September 13, 1970, Raton Quarter Horse Derby.*

*Back in Denver for the Centennial fall race meet, Jet raced to victories in both the Rocky Mountain Quarter Horse Association Derby (top) and the Wonderland Stakes (center). In the Wonderland winner's circle picture (bottom), Walter receives the trophy and congratulations from Colorado great Hugh Bennett.*

**Photos by Ralph Morgan**

*Photographed in the prime of his life, Easy Jet demonstrates the athletic balance and strong bone that enabled him to endure a grueling two-year race career and retire sound.*

**Photo by Orren Mixer**

him off and didn't start him again for three months."

Even with the extended layoff, it took Easy Jet a while to round back into prime running shape. In his next three Ruidoso starts—an August allowance race and the August trials and finals of the World's Championship Classic—he could muster no better than three seconds.

By September, he had regained his competitive edge and the result was a string of five straight wins.

On September 4, he and Willie Lovell raced to a first-place finish in the trials of the 400-yard Raton Derby at La Mesa Park. Nine days later, they won the $25,250 Derby finals by 1½ lengths over Reller and Go Together.

Six weeks later, the pair emerged

victorious in the 440-yard RMQHA Derby trials at Centennial, and on October 4, they duplicated the effort in the finals of the $23,573 stakes event.

On October 25, Easy Jet made his last appearance in the Mile High City, racing to a win over Cinder Leo and Miss Three Wars in the 440-yard Wonderland Stakes.

The stallion's final two starts, in the Sunland Fall Derby trials and finals at Sunland Park in El Paso, Texas, resulted in two more second-place finishes.

The final tally for Easy Jet's sophomore campaign stood at 12 starts, five wins, four seconds and two thirds. His earnings for the year were $36,565 and he was named the 1970 World Champion Stallion and 1970

World Champion Three-Year-Old Colt.

His two-year earnings of $445,720 established an all-time record for a racing Quarter Horse. Nothing remained for the rugged chestnut to prove on the track, and he was officially retired.

But a new race now loomed on the horizon. It would wind up being far more arduous than any Easy Jet experienced on the track. It would involve changes of ownership and places of residence, pathos and pride, controversy and acclaim. Financial milestones would be set and fortunes would be gained and lost—all on Jet's strong back.

But the end result of the second race would be even more impressive than that of the first.

Just as Easy Jet the racehorse rewrote the straightaway record books and raised the bar for all who would follow in his speedy steps, so would Easy Jet the breeding stallion demolish all the existing production records and redefine the standards by which Quarter racing sires would be evaluated from his era forward.

*Even standing still, the legendary stallion is the picture of alert intelligence and pent up energy.*

**Photo by
Orren Mixer**

# 15 JET PROPELLED

*"At around the 300-yard mark, Easy Date's gonna ease up
alongside Easy Six, turn to him and ask, 'How's yo' mama bred?'
And then she's gonna walk off and leave him."
—Walter Merrick, before Easy Date's victory
in the 1974 All-American Futurity*

*The Merrick-bred Easy Jet daughter, Easy Date, was the winner of the 1974 All-American Futurity. The first second-generation horse to accomplish the feat, the bay mare is shown in this Ruidoso Downs portrait with trainer James McArthur and jockey Don Knight.*

THE DUST from Easy Jet's record-setting race career had barely settled before the first offers began pouring in to purchase all or part of him. That they would be forthcoming was understandable.

Jet Deck, Easy Jet's world champion sire and the breed's up-and-coming racehorse progenitor, had died on August 26, 1971—the victim of foul play. Only 11 years old at the time, he had been injected with a massive dose of barbiturates and callously killed by an assailant or assailants unknown. The case was never solved.

This left Easy Jet—Jet Deck's number one son—as both his heir apparent and one of Quarter racing's most lucrative pieces of property.

In the fall of 1971, Walter sold half-interest in both Jet Smooth and Easy

*Spot Cash (TB), Easy Date's dam, was a broke-down racehorse when she caught the eye of Walter Merrick and was tabbed by him to become a Quarter Horse race producer.*

*In December 1974, Easy Date won the rich Sunland Park Futurity in Sunland Park, New Mexico.*

Jet to Houston, Texas, construction contractor Joe McDermott for $500,000. The price was said to be a record at the time, and the partnership was a solid one that worked to both men's advantage through four full breeding seasons.

"Joe McDermott was one of the good guys," Walter says. "He was up front and honest with me from the start, and I never had an ounce of trouble from him for as long as we had business dealings with one another. And Joe went on to become the owner of Raise Your Glass, a top Thoroughbred and the sire of Special Effort."

Two years after the Merrick-McDermott partnership was created, Easy Jet hit the leading sires list for the first time. Based on the accomplishments of his first crop of race-age foals, he was ranked as 1973's sixth-leading sire of money earners, 11th-leading sire of winners–most wins, and 14th-leading sire of winning horses. Jet Deck led all three lists.

The next year, Easy Jet topped his first list as the leading sire of money earners. In 1974, his foals earned $1,393,076, compared to those of second-place Jet Deck, who earned $948,032. As his sons and daughters began raking in the cash on the track, their young sire's stud fee rose proportionately—to $2,500 in 1972, $3,000 in 1973, $5,000 in 1974, and $10,000 in 1975.

By this time, the energy crisis of the early 1970s had given way to the oil and gas production boom years of the mid- to late 1970s. The American economy, particularly in the fossil fuel-producing West, was robust, and oil and gas money was being pumped into the Quarter racing industry at a pace never before witnessed.

The Merrick-McDermott Easy Jet partnership responded by turning out a raft of top-flight runners. Heading the list was a Merrick-bred mare named Easy Date.

"I was at the El Paso racetrack in 1970," Walter says, "when I ran across a nice little Thoroughbred mare named Spot Cash. She'd broke down

*In the All-American, Easy Date eked out a narrow victory over Tiny's Gay and David Capri.*

"EASY DATE"
ALL AMERICAN FUTURITY
(SIXTEENTH RUNNING)
.LTER F. MERRICK, OWNER-JAMES McARTHUR, TR
.0 yds. 21.60 SEPTEMBER 2,1974D.KNIGHT, UP
:NY'S GAY (2nd)        DAVID CAPRI (3rd)
RUIDOSO DOWNS, N.M.

*The 1975 AQHA Champion Running Horse, Easy Date scored big wins in the World Championship Quarter Horse Classic at Ruidoso Downs (left) and The Champion of Champions at Los Alamitos (bottom).*
**Photo courtesy of The Quarter Racing Journal**

on the track, and when I went to inquire about buying her, she was too sore to even stand up.

"I told the fella who owned her that if she ever got well enough to get up, I'd give him $1,500 for her. About a month after the meet was over, he showed up in Sayre with the mare in tow. I paid him and the following spring I bred her to Easy Jet. Easy Date was foaled in 1972."

In the fall of 1973, a young California racehorse trainer named James McArthur paid a visit to Sayre, with hopes of talking Merrick into letting him take some Easy Jet race prospects back to the West Coast to train and campaign.

"I had gotten well-acquainted with James several years earlier," Walter says. "I could see he was a good man, and after he showed up at Sayre and we'd visited for a while, I told him to go into a pen of 20 Easy Jet yearling fillies and pick him out a couple to run.

"So he did. After he'd made his choices, I said to him, 'You've left the runner in the pen.' 'Which one would that be?' he asked. 'The little bay filly with the lop ears,' I said. 'OK, I'll put one of these back and take her instead,' he said."

McArthur probably reflected on that exchange with Walter several times during the ensuing two years, because with McArthur as her trainer, the lop-eared filly—a.k.a. Easy Date—developed into one of the greatest Quarter sprinters of her era.

In 1974, her freshman year on the track, Easy Date totally dominated her competition. The winner of 12 of 13 starts, she raced to victory in the Kindergarten, Miss American, La Chiquata, Sunland Park Fall and All-American futurities. In the latter event, she became the first offspring of an All-American Futurity winner to win the same race.

In the Labor Day extravaganza, she was pitted against Easy Six—a paternal half-brother who would give her all she could handle.

"Easy Six was a Burnett Ranch-bred son of Easy Jet," Walter says. "He was out of Peggy Toro by Hijo The Bull (TB), and he was one tough runner. Coming into the finals of the All-American, both he and Easy Date were undefeated. Easy Six was quick away from the gate, and 'Date' was a great finisher, so I knew we were in for a horse race.

"On the morning of the big race, I was standing outside Easy Date's stall.

*Easy Six, a 1972 stallion by Easy Jet and out of Peggy Toro, wins the 1974 Sun Country Futurity at Sunland Park. Owned by the Burnett Ranch and seemingly destined to be a great sire, the stallion died young.*
**Photo courtesy of**
***The Quarter Racing Journal***

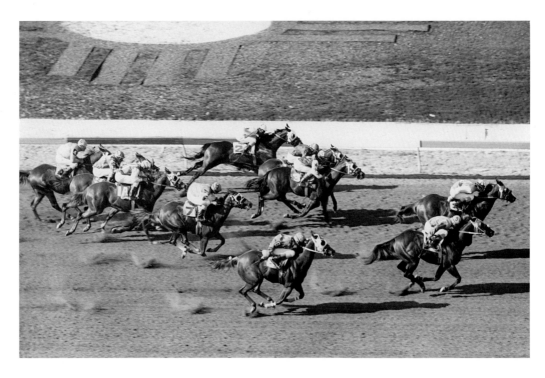

An old horse racing friend of mine stopped by to visit. 'Walt,' he asked, 'what're you gonna do about Easy Six?'

" 'Ain't no way we're gonna beat him out of the gate,' I answered. 'But, at around the 300-yard mark, Easy Date's gonna ease up alongside Easy Six, turn to him and ask, "How's yo' mama bred?" 'And then she's gonna walk off and leave him.' And that's just what she did."

In honor of her five-futurity-winning freshman campaign, Easy Date was named the 1974 World Champion Two-Year-Old Filly.

The next year, the bay Easy Jet daughter returned to the racing wars and emerged victorious in 11 of her 16 starts. The winner of the Rainbow Derby and World's Championship Classic at Ruidoso Downs, the Golden State Derby at Bay Meadows, and Champion of Champions at Los Alamitos, Easy Date closed out her sophomore year with $849,710 in earnings.

She was named the 1975 World Champion, World Champion Mare and World Champion Three-Year-Old Filly, and was retired.

And there were a couple of other Easy Jet champions during the Merrick-McDermott era, as well. The aforementioned Easy Six won the 1974 Sun Country Futurity, the 1975 Kansas Derby, and earned $198,740. Easy Jet Arrive, a 1971 chestnut stallion out of Hialeah Lady by Arrive (TB), achieved a speed index of 96, earned 38 halter and 21 performance points, and was his sire's sole AQHA Champion.

In February of 1976, Merrick and McDermott sold Easy Jet outright to Buena Suerte Ranch of Roswell, New Mexico, for a reported $3.5 million. At the time, it was the richest transaction in the annals of Quarter Horse history. It was also one that set the stage for the first of the major life-altering complications that Walter Merrick and his famous racehorse would suffer through.

"When I decided to sell Easy Jet,"

*Easy Jet Arrive, a 1971 chestnut stallion by Easy Jet and out of Hialeah Lady, achieved a speed index of 96 and was his sire's sole AQHA Champion. He is shown here with 14 Ranch stallion manager Buddy Suthers.*

Walter says, "I retained five breedings each year to him. And three-and-a-half million dollars was a lot to get for a horse. It sure did beat the dollar a day I used to get for putting in a full day's work on the Davis Ranch. So I agreed to the sale. But I had no idea how fast the whole situation would change."

Buena Suerte (Spanish for "Good Luck") was a partnership venture consisting of Grant Brumlow, a banker and insurance executive who owned a ranch near Las Cruces, New Mexico; Harriet Peckham, a noted horsewoman from Roswell; and Leonard Blach, a veterinarian from Roswell. Among the other stallions either owned by the partnership or standing at the ranch were Go Man Go, the three-time world champion

racehorse; Rocket Wrangler; the future sire of Dash For Cash; and Sparkling Native (TB).

The new partners reduced Easy Jet's stud fee from $10,000 to $7,500 and braced themselves for a busy 1976 breeding season. Then, several months into it, Brumlow and his wife, Ethel, were killed in a plane crash, and the entire operation was thrown into a state of financial chaos.

"Looking back," Walter says, "Mr. Brumlow's unexpected death was the first tragedy in a series of events that would impact me and Easy Jet.

"Not long after he died, Harriet began calling me on the phone, asking me to buy up Brumlow's share of Buena Suerte. I didn't really want to do it, but after around the third call I told her that I would—as long as she and Dr. Blach would let me have 51 percent of the whole operation. If I was going to buy into it, I felt I needed to have control.

"She agreed, so I made the financial arrangements, assumed the majority interest of the entire operation, and sent my son Joe out there to help run things."

For several years, the arrangement seemed a viable one. The economy continued to boom and the Quarter racing industry continued to flourish. Buena Suerte was a mecca for the affluent short horse set, and was the scene of not only industry-leading breeding activity, but several lavishly catered, exclusive bloodstock sales as well.

And Easy Jet was the acknowledged superstar of Buena Suerte's star-studded stallion battery. As his sons and daughters began to dominate the Quarter racing scene, his stud fee climbed to the unheard-of mark of $20,000.

The fee was an easy one to justify, however. The prepotent stallion's sons and daughters did it for him on a year-in, year-out basis. Among the brightest Easy Jet stars during the Buena Suerte era were Megahertz, My Easy Credit, Easy Move, Real Easy Jet, Easy Angel, Extra Easy, Pie In The Sky and Easily Smashed.

*Megahertz, a 1974 bay stallion by Easy Jet and out of Lady Meyers, was the 1976 World Champion 2-Year-Old Colt.*

**Photo courtesy of**
*The Quarter Racing Journal*

Megahertz, a 1974 bay stallion out of Lady Meyers by Mr Meyers, earned $160,773 and was the 1976 World Champion Two-Year-Old Colt.

My Easy Credit, a 1974 sorrel stallion out of Kits Charge Acct by Diamond Charge, earned $502,504. Trained by Walter as a 3-year-old, he became the first horse to win the Quarter Horse Triple Crown—the Kansas, Rainbow and All-American Derbies. He was also named the 1977 World Champion Three-Year-Old and World Champion Three-Year-Old Colt.

Easy Move, a 1975 bay stallion out of To The Front by Clabber II, won the 1978 Kansas Derby, earned $140,553 and was the 1978 World Champion Three-Year-Old Colt.

The year 1979 was a banner one for the Easy Jet freshman runners. Pie In The Sky, a 1977 brown stallion out of Miss Jelly Roll by Roulade (TB), won the All-American Futurity, earned $616,328, and was named the 1979 World Champion Two-Year-Old Colt.

Likewise, Easy Angel, a 1977 sorrel mare out of Alamitos Angel by Alamitos Bar, won the Kindergarten and Skoal Dash For Cash futurities, earned $477,634 and was the 1979 AQHA World Champion Two-Year-Old and World Champion Two-Year-Old Filly.

Easily Smashed, a 1978 sorrel stallion out of Smash It (TB) by Foggy Road, won the Sun Country Futurity and the Kansas Derby, earned $326,060, and was the 1981 World Champion Three-Year-Old Colt.

*Walter Merrick, My Easy Credit and jockey Gary Sumpter pose in the infield at Ruidoso Downs in 1977. That year, the trio became the first ever to win the Quarter Horse Triple Crown—the Kansas, Rainbow and All-American Derbies.*

And then there was the Merrick-bred speedster Real Easy Jet. Although never a world champion runner, the 1975 sorrel stallion did win the 1977 Oklahoma Futurity and earn $153,833. He also enjoys the distinction of being one of the fastest racehorses his breeder can ever recall training.

"Real Easy Jet was out of Real Dish, a Thoroughbred mare sired by Royal Charger," Walter says. "I bought her from Melvin Hatley of Norman, Oklahoma, and she was one of the best-made Thoroughbred mares I ever owned.

"Real Easy Jet was her best foal, and he was a pure runner. In fact, he could run so fast he'd scare you. But he was also temperamental. He won his trial heat in just about every stakes race we ever entered him in, but then he seldom seemed to give the same kind of effort in the finals. So he only

won the one futurity. If he'd had anything that was close to his daddy's consistency as a runner, there's no telling what he could have accomplished."

In addition to the impressive collection of Easy Jet-sired world champion runners owned by Buena Suerte, there were a number of other noteworthy racehorses as well. They included:

- Easy Treasure, four-time stakes winner and earner of $361,748.
- Prissy Gold Digger, five-time stakes winner, and earner of $299,590.
- Love N Money, five-time stakes winner and earner of $272,116.
- Flamboyan, stakes winner and earner of $268,851.
- Easy Della Jet, six-time stakes winner and earner of $223,726.
- Sunset Gallant Jet, stakes winner and 1979 and 1980 AQHA High-Point Cutter and Chariot Horse.

*Easy Move, a 1975 bay stallion by Easy Jet and out of To The Front, went to the post in the 1978 Kansas Quarter Horse Derby as a 13-to-1 long shot. Confounding the odds-makers, he scored an impressive 1¼-length victory.*

**Photo courtesy of**
*The Quarter Racing Journal*

By the 1980 season, the breeding fee for Easy Jet had skyrocketed to $30,000. Late that year, the then-13-year-old stallion changed ownership for the fourth time. And, although it wasn't apparent at the onset, this move would wind up being a total train wreck.

In a deal concocted by Oklahoma bloodstock agency agent Don Tyner, Easy Jet was syndicated in late 1980 for the then-world-record price of $30 million. By comparison, the Thoroughbred stallion Spectacular Bid had been syndicated earlier in the year for a record $20 million.

The Easy Jet syndicate involved 50 shares at $600,000 each—with each share entitling the owner to four breedings per year. Buena Suerte opted to keep 26 shares, and the rest were quickly snapped up. Easy Jet remained in Roswell, and for several years things proceeded in an orderly manner. The economy was still robust, the horse business was still flourishing and everyone seemed content.

Then, in 1982, the bubble burst. Seemingly overnight, the gas and oil industry ground to a screeching halt. Texas and Oklahoma—home of the majority of syndicate members—were particularly hard hit.

In Walter's own town of Sayre, long-established businesses were forced to shut their doors, and at one point the city itself had to turn off every other street light so it could afford to pay its electric bill. The cattle market crashed and the horse market soon followed. The entire country lay firmly in the grip of a major recession.

The Easy Jet syndicate was in no better shape. Some of the members wanted out, while others simply refused to make their payments. In frustration, the Buena Suerte combine—Merrick, Pecham and Blach—were forced to trade out with a number of share-holders, giving them their money back in the form of breedings.

The situation worsened. In early 1982, controlling interest in both Easy Jet and his son Real Easy Jet—who had been acquired by Buena Suerte several years earlier—was bought up by League Inc., a Dallas-based oil company owned and operated by Richard Wolfe.

Wolfe and Blach had a falling-out, and Wolfe attempted to move Easy Jet to a farm he owned in Purcell, Oklahoma. Walter would not agree to

*Pie In The Sky, a 1977 brown stallion by Easy Jet and out of Miss Jelly Roll, became the second of his sire's get to win the All-American Futurity when he sped to an easy victory in the 1979 edition of the Quarter racing classic.*
**Photo courtesy of**
***The Quarter Racing Journal***

the move and returned Jet to Sayre to stand the 1983 and 1984 seasons.

After putting in the neighborhood of $1 million down on a total debt obligation of $15½ million, Wolfe defaulted on his agreement. League Inc. filed for Chapter 11 bankruptcy protection in October of 1984, and the ownership of Easy Jet was once again cast into a state of limbo.

Through it all—and despite the fact that the cloudy financial picture that surrounded him drove many would-be breeders off—the famed Quarter Horse stallion continued to prove that he was the breed's most potent sire of speed.

From his 1982, 1983 and 1984 foal crops came such sprinting luminaries as Mr Trucka Jet, winner of the 1985 All-American Futurity and the earner of $1,033,115, and Stars In Her Crown, stakes winner and the earner of $217,757.

By the fall of 1984, Easy Jet was the most prolific active race sire on the North American continent. His 110 stakes winners and earners of $17,302,319, ranked him ahead of such noteworthy Thoroughbred sires as Northern Dancer, Nijinsky II and Mr. Prospector.

*Easy Angel, a 1977 sorrel mare by Easy Jet and out of Alamitos Angel, was a two-time world champion racehorse and the earner of $477,634.*

**Photos courtesy of** *The Quarter Racing Journal*

By this time, the Buena Suerte combine had been expanded to include Melvin Hatley of Norman, Oklahoma. In 1985, Easy Jet stood under Hatley's management at Dee and Betty Raper's Belle Mere Farms in Lexington, Oklahoma, for a $15,000 fee. It was reported that he was bred to 114 mares that season.

In 1986 and 1987, he was returned to Merrick and stood both seasons at Sayre. And still the Easy Jet runners just kept coming. Among them were:

- Teller Queen, a five-time stakes winner and the earner of $637,917.
- Shoot Yeah, the 1987 World Champion Two-Year-Old Colt, a stakes winner and the earner of $304,143.
- Freedom Flyer, stakes winner and the earner of $309,008.
- Mighty Easy Pass, stakes winner and the earner of $278,825.
- Some Power Play, the earner of $203,163.

In October of 1987, Easy Jet was purchased by Roi Young and moved to Gateway Farms in Hemet, California. He stood the 1988 season for a stud fee of $10,000 and was reportedly bred to 200 mares. For the 1989 season, Young relocated Gateway

*Seen here are two more world champion Easy Jet sprinters. Extra Easy (top), a 1978 sorrel stallion out of Hempen Will (TB), was the 1980 World Champion 2-Year-Old Colt, while Easily Smashed, a 1978 sorrel stallion out of Smash It (TB), was the 1981 World Champion 3-Year-Old Colt.*

In 1974, Walter bred the Quarter-built Thoroughbred mare Real Dish (top) to Easy Jet. The cross resulted in Real Easy Jet (bottom), a sorrel stallion who his breeder claims was one of the fastest sprinters he ever trained.

"REAL EASY JET"
KANSAS FUTURITY TRIALS
WALTER P. MERRICK, OWNER & TR
350 yds. 17.94 MAY 19, 1977 G. SUMPTER, UP
PROMISE OF JOY (2nd)          HIJO THE MAN (3rd)
TWELFTH DIVISION          RUIDOSO DOWNS, N.M.

Farms and the then-22-year-old Easy Jet to Jacksboro, Texas. There, the aging stallion's book was reportedly limited to 80 mares.

Still, bad fortune continued to haunt the now-legendary sire. Young had apparently used Easy Jet and other items to collateralize some big-money loans. In October of 1988, the stallion was supposed to sell in a court-ordered sheriff's sale. The incident was averted when Young and his wife reportedly filed for Chapter 11 bankruptcy protection.

In September of 1989, Easy Jet changed hands again. Bill Allen, an oil service operator from Anchorage, Alaska, purchased the stallion from the Federal Bankruptcy Court for an undisclosed price. He was returned to the 14 Ranch in Sayre to stand there under the joint control of Merrick and

Allen for the 1990 and 1991 seasons.

In May of 1991, ownership of Jet was transferred to Mark Allen, Bill Allen's son. The stallion was relocated to the Lazy E Ranch in Guthrie, Oklahoma, to stand the 1992 season.

On May 6, 1992, Easy Jet's epic race into Quarter Horse history finally came to an end. Suffering from the effects of chronic laminitis (founder), he was humanely put to sleep at the age of 25. As had been agreed upon by Walter and Bill Allen, his remains were promptly returned to Sayre, to be laid to rest there.

When it was all said and done, Easy Jet's record as a sire was one for the ages.

AQHA records reveal that he sired 2,505 foals. Of those, 2,024 were performers. As racehorses, 2,019 have been starters. They have amassed

*As this picture of Real Easy Jet's winning effort in the 1977 Kansas Futurity trials graphically shows, when he was on, the Easy Jet son could "run off and hide" from the competition. Despite this fact, he proved inconsistent and won only one stakes final during his two-year racing career.*

1,563 race ROMs and 864 have achieved speed indexes of 90 or above. They have also accounted for 112 Superior Race awards, 14 world championships and earned $26,231,441.

Through 2000, he remained the number one all-time leading sire of ROM qualifiers and the number three all-time leading sire of money earners.

As a maternal grandsire, the Merrick-bred stallion's record is even more amazing.

To date, Easy Jet's daughters have produced 5,927 AQHA-registered foals. Of these, 3,797 have been performers. As racehorses, 3,740 have been starters. They have earned 2,556 ROMs and 1,376 have achieved speed indexes of 90 or above. They have earned 143 Superior Race awards, 13 world championships and $43,057,329.

Through the year 2000, Easy Jet stood alone as the number one all-time leading broodmare sire of ROM qualifiers and the number one all-time leading broodmare sire of money earners.

Among the prepotent stallion's top maternal grandget are:
• Eastex, 1984 World Champion Two-Year-Old and World Champion Two-Year-Old Gelding, winner of the 1986 All-American Futurity, four-time stakes winner and earner of $1,869,406.
• Make Mine Cash, three-time stakes winner and earner of $1,142,428.
• Takin On The Cash, 1990 World Champion Two-Year-Old Colt, 1991 World Champion Two-Year-Old and World Champion Three-Year-Old Colt, eight-time stakes winner and the earner of $661,697.
• Meganette, two-time stakes winner and earner of $657,620.
• Dashing Perfection, five-time stakes winner and earner of $553,644.
• Rise N High, 1984 World Champion Three-Year-Old Gelding, seven-time stakes winner and earner of $522,075.
• Such An Easy Effort, six-time stakes winner and earner of $496,127.
• Easygo Effort, seven-time stakes winner and earner of $432,551.
• Lucks Easyfanta Boy, AQHA Supreme Champion.

Still, according to his breeder and trainer, the Easy Jet story remains, to a certain extent, one of "what might have been."

*As a racehorse, Prissy Gold Digger—a 1975 sorrel mare by Easy Jet and out of Broom Straw—won five stakes and earned $299,590. As an all-time leading dam of race ROMs, she produced such stars as Diggin For Gold ($426,086) and Awesome Blossom ($118,511).*

**Photos courtesy of**
***The Quarter Racing Journal***

*Shoot Yeah, a 1985 sorrel stallion by Easy Jet out of Little Tiny Lamb, was the 1987 World Champion 2-Year-Old Colt. He earned $304,143.*
**Photos courtesy of The Quarter Racing Journal**

OWNER WALTER MERRICK  ☆ STUB ☆  TRAINER JOE MERRICK
JOCKEY DANNY CARDOZA  MAY 28, 1980  LOS ALAMITOS RACE COURSE
Fair Trip (2nd)  400 yds-20.17  PURSE $4200  My Fortune Cookie (3rd)

*Stub, a 1977 bay full brother to Easy Date, won six of his 21 starts and was slated to take his place as a 14 Ranch herd sire before his untimely death as a 3-year-old. Trainer Joe Merrick is at the far right in this winner's circle photo.*

Coda Mundi, a 1979 chestnut stallion by Easy Jet and out of Olivia by Hempen (TB), was the winner of five stakes events and $105,278.
**Photo courtesy of The Quarter Racing Journal**

With $1,869,406 to his credit, Eastex, a 1982 brown gelding by Texas Dancer (TB) and out of Tall Cotton, ranks as Easy Jet's top money-earning maternal grandget.
**Photo courtesy of The Quarter Racing Journal**

*Takin On The Cash, a 1988 sorrel stallion by Dash For Cash and out of Take You On by Easy Jet, was a three-time world champion and the earner of $661,697.*
**Photo courtesy of**
*The Quarter Racing Journal*

*Dashing Perfection, a 1994 sorrel gelding by First Down Dash and out of Perfect Arrangement by Easy Jet, was a two-time world champion and earned $553,644.*
**Photo courtesy of**
*The Quarter Racing Journal*

*Meganette, a 1981 bay mare by Dash For Cash and out of Easy Secret, won the Rainbow Futurity, Rainbow Silver Cup, and earned $657,620.*
**Photo courtesy of *The Quarter Racing Journal***

*Although not noted as a halter sire, Easy Jet did manage to turn out some well-made foals. Spotted Easy, a 1972 sorrel stallion by Easy Jet and out of Spot It (TB) by Spotted Bull, earned 15 open halter points.*
**Photo by Alfred Janssen Ill, courtesy of *The Quarter Horse Journal***

"Easy Jet was mismanaged a lot during his breeding career," Walter says. "To begin with, I have to assume most of the blame. I was never anything but a cowboy, and I was capable of seeing stars. I was blinded by all the money that people started throwing at me in the early 1980s, and I allowed those people to turn my head and make some decisions that I shouldn't have.

"There were a lot of people that climbed on the Easy Jet bandwagon that never should have been allowed to. They weren't horse people to begin with, and they weren't people who kept their word. At the first sign of trouble, all they could think about was jumping off and saving their own hides.

"Later, when I had for all practical purposes lost control of Jet, some other people stepped in for very questionable reasons. Whether they did so to just exploit him, or to gain some sort of notoriety by being connected with him we'll never know. But Easy Jet suffered because of it.

"If he hadn't been mismanaged—hadn't come under the control of people of questionable financial stability who constantly shuffled him around—there's no telling how great a sire he might have been.

"Still, he made a pretty good one. And I know I'll always be proud that I bred and owned him, thankful that he was a part of my life, and grateful for what he did for me and my family.

"Easy Jet was a once-in-a-lifetime racehorse, and a once-in-a-lifetime sire. And he never dropped the ball on anyone."

*Boundaway Easy, a 1973 chestnut stallion out of Miss Bound Away, earned a 93 speed index and placed third in the Aged Stallion class at the 1978 AQHA World Show.*
**Photo courtesy of**
*The Quarter Horse*
*Journal*

# 16 RIPPLED WATER

*"That part never changes I guess. And who knows,*
*maybe one of these colts will win the All-American for me."*
—Walter Merrick

*Good Bird, a 1956 chestnut stallion by Papa Red Bird and out of Goody by*
*Menow, was one of a number of good-looking "post-Three Bars"*
*Thoroughbreds to be used as sires by Walter Merrick.*

**Photo by Orren Mixer**

THROUGHOUT THE Easy Jet years—dating back to the stallion's birth in 1967 and continuing until his death in 1992—Walter Merrick stood and promoted other speed-bred stallions, trained and raced straightaway runners for himself and others, and incorporated the blood of both sets of horses into his already potent breeding program.

And, just as it had when he introduced Three Bars into the Quarter Horse mainstream a decade-and-a-half earlier, the impact of the venerable horseman's efforts on both the breeding and racing fronts reverberated throughout the industry.

The first major echo came as a result of his mid-1960 acquisition of Good Bird, a 1956 chestnut Thoroughbred stallion sired by Papa Red Bird and out of Goody by Menow.

"I bought Good Bird from John T. L. Jones in the fall of 1966," Walter says. "Johnny had always had a good eye for a horse and he was a serious student of Thoroughbred bloodlines and performance, as well. And after he left this country, he went on to found Walmac Stud, one of the premiere Thoroughbred breeding establishments in Kentucky.

"Like Three Bars, Good Bird was a stakes-winning racehorse and had excellent Quarter Horse conformation.

"*Laico Bird*"

"THE RATON QUARTER HORSE FUTURITY $111,861.16"

LA MESA PARK, N.M.          JULY 30, 1967          B. HARMON, UP
SHOWMAN'S SQUAW (2nd)       400 Yds 19.77          ASTROJET (3rd)
FLOYD H. JONES, OWNER                       JIMMY R.B.JONES, TRAINER

*Among Good Bird's first noteworthy get was Laico Bird, a 1965 brown mare out of Paula Laico. A three-time world champion racehorse, she won the 1967 All-American Futurity and earned $435,653.*

He was an above-average sire of early speed, and I stood him to the public for a number of years."

Walter's decision to purchase Good Bird and stand him alongside Three Bars in Quannah, Texas, was just one more example of the Oklahoma horseman's intuitive feel for the Quarter racing game.

The very year he linked his name with that of the good-looking Thoroughbred stallion, Laico Bird, a 1965 brown daughter of Good Bird and out of Paula Laico by Laico (TB), won the All-American, Los Alamitos, Raton, Texas and Columbus futurities, as well as the Buttons and Bows Stakes. She then went on to be named 1967 World Champion, World

Champion Mare, World Champion 2-Year-Old Filly, and earn $435,653 during a two-year racing career.

Over the course of the next three years, Good Bird sired a number of additional top runners, including Good Bird Bars, stakes winner and earner of $41,263; Mystery Bird, two-time stakes winner; Pine's Birdie, two-time stakes winner; Good Baldy Bar, two-time stakes winner; and King Bird, stakes winner.

Byou Bird, the stallion's final track superstar, arrived courtesy of the Merrick breeding program.

"Byou Bird was a 1970 chestnut mare out of Delta Rose, my best-looking Tonto Bars Hank–Lena's Bar daughter," Walter says. "Unlike

*Byou Bird, a 1970 chestnut mare by Good Bird and out of Delta Rose by Tonto Bars Hank, was the 1972 World Champion 2-Year-Filly, won four futurities and earned $309,643. In this shot, Benjamin Franklin and Walter stand at Byou Bird's head, while Elbert Minchey is in the saddle.*

*I Get By, a 1976 sorrel stallion by Easy Jet and out of Byou Bird, achieved a speed index of 92 and won the 1979 Raton Futurity at La Mesa Park.*

'Rose,' 'Bird' wasn't very big and didn't have a very pretty head. But she was a pure runner."

As a 2-year-old, Byou Bird pulled off victories in the Blue Ribbon, West Texas, Kansas and Oklahoma Futurities, and was named the 1972 World Champion 2-Year-Old Filly. In two seasons on the track, she earned $309,643.

"Even though Good Bird was an above-average breeding horse," Walter says, "he wasn't as consistent a sire as Three Bars or Easy Jet. Still, he did me and a bunch of other folks some good, and I was glad to have had the opportunity to use him."

Throughout the early to mid-1970s, spurred on by the positive impact that both Three Bars and Good Bird had on his breeding and race programs, Walter continued to search for another top-notch Thoroughbred to stand.

Among the stallions he tried out during that era were Venetian Jester, Jackstraw Jr and Cherokee Arrow.

Venetian Jester and Jackstraw Jr, while probably two of the most beautifully conformed stallions that Walter ever stood, were average as sires of speed.

Cherokee Arrow was a more consistent sire of speed, but still failed to suit the Oklahoma horseman well enough to earn him a permanent spot on the 14 Ranch stallion roster.

Then, in the mid-1970s, the Thoroughbred stallion who would prove to be the perfect fit was located and imported.

*Venetian Jester (TB), a royally bred son of Tom Fool, out of Venice by Princequillo, was unquestionably one of the most beautiful Thoroughbred stallions to ever be utilized by Walter Merrick.*

"By that time," Walter says, "Johnny Jones had moved to Kentucky. We kept in touch, though, and I had asked him to keep his eye out for a stallion. Johnny knew the kind of horse I was looking for, and in the fall of 1976 he called and said he'd found one he thought I'd like.

"His name was Hempen, and next to Three Bars, he probably did my program as much good as any Thoroughbred I ever used."

Hempen, a 1962 chestnut stallion by Indian Hemp and out of Serry by Spy Song, was a four-time stakes winner and the earner of $108,808. Blessed with well-balanced Quarter Horse conformation, he was also a horse of proven early speed.

After purchasing him in 1976, Walter syndicated the then-15-year-old stallion and stood him in Sayre from 1977 through 1983. His impact on not only Walter's program, but the Quarter

racing industry as well, was profound.

AQHA records reveal that Hempen sired 806 Quarter Horse foals. Of these, 651 were performers and they amassed three world championships, 62 Superior Race awards, 513 ROMs, 278 speed indexes of 90 or above, and earned $7,338,365. Among his most noteworthy sprinting stars were:
• Rise N High, seven-time stakes winner, the earner of $522,075, and 1984 World Champion 3-Year-Old Gelding.
• Liberty Coin, two-time stakes winner, the earner of $291,799, and 1988 World Champion 2-Year-Old Gelding.
• Im Gorgeous, stakes winner, the earner of $178,058, and 1976 World Champion 2-Year-Old Filly.
• The Shogun, four-time stakes winner and the earner of $374,052.
• Hempens Jet, two-time stakes winner and the earner of $271,083.

*Here is Hempen (TB), a 1962 chestnut stallion by Indian Hemp and out of Serry by Spy Song. Next to Three Bars and Easy Jet, Hempen had the most positive impact on Walter Merrick's speed breeding program.*
**Photo by** *Speedhorse*

*In this shot taken in the early 1980s at the 14 Ranch headquarters near Sayre, Hempen enjoys a little play time.*
**Photo by**
***The Quarter Horse Journal***

*Liberty Coin, a 1986 sorrel gelding by Hempen and out of Cherished Lady by Easy Jet, scores a victory in the Ed Burke Memorial Futurity at Los Alamitos. The Merrick-bred speedster was the 1988 World Champion 2-Year-Old Gelding and earned $291,799.*
**Photo courtesy of**
***The Quarter Racing Journal***

- Mr Easy Ed, three-time stakes winner and the earner of $230,332.
- Summer Encounter, the earner of $221,623.
- Hempeasy Girl, two-time stakes winner and the earner of $218,603.
- Hempens Double, AQHA Champion.

And, like Easy Jet, Hempen's contributions as a broodmare sire were also very impressive.

AQHA records show that the daughters of Hempen have produced 1,923 Quarter Horse foals to date. Of these, 1,180 have been performers. They have amassed 10 world championships, 41 Superior Race awards, 767 ROMs, 448 speed indexes of 90 or above, and earned $12,160,929. Among his most accomplished grandget are:

- Separatist, seven-time stakes winner, the earner of $889,044, 1999 World Champion 2-Year-Old Colt, 2000 World Champion 3-Year-Old and World Champion 3-Year-Old Colt.
- Way Maker, four-time stakes winner, the earner of $617,444, and 1989 World Champion 2-Year-Old Gelding.
- Dashing Folly, nine-time stakes winner, the earner of $535,841, 1996 World Champion, World Champion 3-Year-Old, World Champion 3-Year-Old Mare, and 1997 World Champion Aged Mare.
- Extra Easy, two-time stakes winner, the earner of $165,105, and 1980 World Champion 3-Year-Old Colt.

After Hempen, Walter stood the Thoroughbred stallion Raise Caine from 1981 through 1984.

The Oklahoma horseman's commitment to the judicious use of Thoroughbred blood to produce world-caliber Quarter Horse runners did not mean he ignored his Quarter stallions.

Throughout the 1970s and 1980s, Easy Jet was Walter's mainstay as a racehorse sire, and the stallion's maternal half-brothers Jet Smooth and Double Dancer also figured prominently in the 14 Ranch breeding program.

Additionally, over the course of the same two decades, Walter either stood or bred to a number of Easy Jet's top sons, including Easy Jet Arrive, Real Easy Jet, My Easy Credit, Easy Move, Arrivin Easy Jet, Stub and Codi Mundi.

No matter which stallion he chose to stand or breed to, though, when he did so the rest of the Quarter racing world stood up and took notice.

*Dashing Folly, a 1993 sorrel mare by Dash For Cash and out of Hempes Folly by Hempen was a four-time world champion, won nine stakes events and earned $535,841. In addition to being a daughter of Hempen, Dashing Folly's dam, Hempes Folly is a granddaughter of Easy Jet and a great granddaughter of Bob's Folly.*

**Photo courtesy of** *The Quarter Racing Journal*

"CHICKAMONA"
"THE JODY MILLER PURSE"

LA MESA PARK, N.M.        MAY 20, 1967        W. LOVELL, UP
ROSE OF DIAMONDS (2nd)    350 Yds 17.86        BAR POTEET (3rd
WALTER MERRICK, LESSEE                    PHIL GARRETT, TRAINE
CHICKAMONA SYNDICATE, LESSOR

*By the mid-1960s, Walter Merrick was very much in demand as a racehorse trainer. In 1966 and 1967, he leased Chicamona, a 1964 mare by Triple Chick and out of Monita, to race. The fleet filly placed second in both the 1966 All-American and Raton Futurities and earned more than $100,000.*

*In 1977, Walter trained and campaigned both My Easy Credit (top) and Real Wind (bottom) to world champion 3-year-old honors.*

Walter's stamp of approval on any stallion was often all it took for that horse to become an instant breeding success.

And despite the murky financial water that often surrounded Easy Jet, the Merrick 14 Ranch remained one of the breeding epicenters of the Quarter racehorse world. The operation was a vast one, with Walter's son-in-law, Buddy Suthers, filling the role of ranch manager and his youngest daughter, Lynnie Merrick Suthers, running the office. In addition, Fred Rule served for years as ranch veterinarian.

But standing stallions and raising race prospects was not all that occupied Walter's time. By now, he was one of the most renowned Quarter racehorse trainers of all time, and top-flight runners from throughout the West were brought to him to condition and campaign. Three of the very best were Chickamona, Real Wind and My Easy Credit.

*By the late 1970s, Walter Merrick had progressed from being a dollar-a-day Depression-era cowboy, to a rancher with widespread holdings and his own personal airplane to take him to horse races and cattle brandings.*

*Shake The Bank, a 1982 sorrel mare by Bully Bullion and out of Shake Em Six by Streakin Six, was a three-time world champion, a five-time stakes winner and earned $368,025.*

**Photo courtesy of** *The Quarter Racing Journal*

"Up until Easy Jet," Walter says, "the closest I ever came to winning the All-American Futurity was with Chickamona. She was a 1964 mare by Triple Chick and out of Monita. I never did own the mare, but I leased and ran her in 1966 and 1967.

"In 1966, she ran second by a head to Go Dick Go in the All-American, second in the Raton Futurity, and earned more than $100,000. After she was retired, she went on to produce several good runners. Her best was probably an Easy Jet daughter named Easy Blush, who was a futurity winner and the earner of $35,000."

Real Wind and My Easy Credit fared a little better than Chickamona as members of Walter's 14 Ranch race string.

"I had Real Wind and My Easy Credit in my stable at the same time," Walter says. "The year was 1977, and they were both 3-year-olds.

"Real Wind had won the All-American the year before, and was the World Champion 2-Year-Old. So I was delighted when her owners, Mr. and Mrs. J. D. Kitchens of Ft. Sumner, New Mexico, asked me to campaign her as a 3-year-old."

"Real Wind had some real interesting breeding," he continues. "She was sired by Go With The Wind, a son of Go Man Go who was out of a Three Bars and Papa Red Bird-bred mare. On the bottom, Real Wind was out of Real New, by Golly, and Golly was a son of Leo out of Sheelgo, the first AAA-rated mare I ever trained.

"In 1977, Real Wind won the West Texas Derby at Sunland Park, as well as several other races. She also qualified for her Superior Racehorse award that year, and was the World Champion 3-Year-Old Filly.

"At the end of the year, the Kitchens retired the mare, and the following spring, bred her to Easy Jet. She had a nice colt in 1979 named Real Jet Wind. He won more than $100,000 on the tracks, but he was the mare's only foal. She died young."

As well as Real Wind did for Walter in 1977, the nod for the star of the year still had to go to My Easy Credit.

"My Easy Credit was owned by Harold Burford of Milton, Kansas," Walter says. "He was a nice-looking sorrel stallion by Easy Jet and out of Kits Charge Acct by Diamond Charge. I'd seen him run as a 2-year-old, and

*Royal Shake Em, a 1994 Merrick-bred gray stallion by Royal Quick Dash and out of Shake Em Six, was a two-time stakes winner and earned $257,009.*

**Photo courtesy of Double S Farm**

" LOQUENDI "
KANSAS FUTURITY TRIALS
WALTER F. MERRICK, OWNER & TR
350 yds. 17.950      MAY 18, 1985        C. LAMBERT, UP
EASY RAISE (2nd)                         MS MAZZARTI RULER  (3rd)
TWENTY-FIRST DIVISION                    RUIDOSO DOWNS, N.M.

while he hadn't gotten much done that year, I could see he was a runner. I talked Mr. Burford into letting me train him as a 3-year-old, and the colt and I just sorta clicked.

"In 1977," he continues, "My Easy Credit became the first horse to ever win the Quarter Horse Triple Crown—the Kansas Derby, Rainbow Derby and All-American Derby. And he was named the World Champion 3-Year-Old and World Champion 3-Year-Old Colt. His total race earnings amounted to $502,504.

"In 1978, I stood My Easy Credit at stud at my ranch. He looked like he was going to make a breeding horse, but he never got a chance to prove it. Mr. Burford moved him to another place in Oklahoma for the 1979 breeding season, and he died there as the result of a spill he took on a sheet of ice.

"So neither Real Wind or My Easy Credit lived very long. But I was sure proud I had them in my stable in 1977, and they made the year a pretty enjoyable one for me."

By the mid-1970s, the ripple effect of Walter Merrick's breeding and race training successes extended into a third area, as well.

That area was ranching.

Flushed with the financial proceeds of first, the $3.5 million sale of Easy Jet to Buena Suerte, and second, the $30 million syndication of him, Walter began aggressively expanding his ranching operations.

Between 1976 and 1980, the former dollar-a-day cowboy purchased two additional ranches in Oklahoma, one in New Mexico, one in South Dakota and one in Montana. The New Mexico and Montana spreads were

*Loquendi, a 1983 sorrel mare by L'Natural (TB) and out of Talking Picture by Easy Jet, is a current member of the Merrick broodmare band. The good-looking runner won the 1985 Rocket Bar Futurity and earned $54,351.*

particularly large—totaling more than 100,000 acres each of deeded and BLM-leased land.

Walter's oldest son, Jim, now in his mid-40s, was dispatched to oversee the 4,000-acre South Dakota operation. Son-in-law and daughter, Bob and Donna Moss, assumed control of the 12-section Beaver, Oklahoma, ranch—an operation that concentrated on putting up thousands of bales of prime alfalfa hay.

Outside managers where brought in to oversee the remaining ranches.

Walter and his 14 Ranch—which had been started in the late 1930s with a $750 insurance policy and a $300 black Quarter Horse stallion—was now literally an empire. There was even a summer home in Ruidoso to retreat to, and a Cheyenne II twin-engine corporate airplane to transport Walter and his family between the racetracks and ranches.

But, just as the recession of the early 1980s served to put the dampers on the Quarter Horse racing industry in general, and the Easy Jet syndicate in particular, so did it bring the cattle ranching industry and everything connected to it to a screeching halt.

Overnight, land values plummeted and the cattle market hit rock bottom. The decision was made to cut back and regroup and, over the course of the next decade, the majority of the Merrick land holdings were put on the market and sold. By the early 1990s, only the Crawford and Sayre operations remained.

As he had always done when the times were tough, Walter regrouped and began looking for new ways to succeed.

In the late 1980s, Oklahoma and Texas passed legislation legalizing

*The beautiful Sweet Illusion, a 1985 sorrel mare by Easy Jet and out of Mayflower Moon by Top Moon, was both a top runner and producer.*

*Sweet Advice, a 1993 bay mare by Bully Bullion and out of Sweet Illusion, fared well on the tracks and looks to make her mark as a 14 Ranch broodmare, as well. Walter's grandson Destry Suthers was the mare's trainer in this 1996 win at the Ellis County Fairgrounds in Arnett, Oklahoma.*

pari-mutuel racetrack betting. Both Buddy Suthers and Joe Merrick had been long-time students of Thoroughbred breeding and racing, and Joe had also become a successful racehorse trainer.

In 1990, with Easy Jet near the end of his life and no top-notch Quarter Horse replacement for him in sight, the decision was made to import four Thoroughbred stallions from Kentucky.

That they were first-class individuals was never an issue. Vanlandingham, a 1981 bay stallion by Cox's Ridge and out of Populi, was the six-time stakes winner of $1,409,476. Track Barron, a 1981 brown stallion by Buckfinder and out of golden Spike, was a seven-time stakes winner of $1,353,674. Highland Blade, a 1978 brown stallion by Damascus and out of Misty Bryn, was a six-time stakes winner of $998,888. And Garthon, a 1980 brown stallion by Believe It and out of Garden Verse, was a six-time stakes winner of $732,393. All four stallions were multi-million-dollar sires.

On the surface, and based on the sense of optimism and enthusiasm that accompanied the arrival of new

*Sweetly Special, a 1990 sorrel mare by Special Effort and out of Sweet Illusion achieved a speed index of 101. Here, she races to victory in a 1993 350-yard contest at Remington Park in Oklahoma City.*

race plants and legalized betting in the Southwest, the shift in emphasis seemed a prudent move.

In retrospect, it was probably one that was initiated a decade too soon.

As it had been from the days of the Sooner Land Rush, western Oklahoma was "short horse" country. The regional racehorse men were knowledgeable when it came to sprinting Quarter Horse sires, but slightly less so when it came to classic Thoroughbred sires.

And because the Jockey Club doesn't allow artificial insemination or shipped semen, there was no East or West Coast business to be had. By the end of the decade, most of the Kentucky Thoroughbreds had been dispersed.

As the new century dawned, Walter Merrick had essentially come full circle as a horse breeder, and found himself at a point very similar to the one he had started from six decades earlier.

His 14 Ranch program was once again an operation that had as its heart a small, select band of mares. With the exception of one Thoroughbred, they were all Easy Jet and Midnight Jr-bred. Most had proven their mettle on the track, and all had the genetic strength to transmit their speed.

Shake Em Six, a Merrick-owned 1982 daughter of Streakin Six by Easy Six, was one of the breed's premiere producers. A top race mare in her own right, with a speed index of 97,

she was also named the 1996 Broodmare of the Year. The award came in recognition of the accomplishments of two of her Walter Merrick-bred offspring:

- Shake The Bank, a 1993 sorrel mare by Bully Bullion, five-time stakes winner, second in the 1995 All-American Futurity, the earner of $368,025, the 1995 World Champion 2-Year-Old Filly, and the 1996 Mexico Champion Racing Quarter Horse and Mexico Champion 3-Year-Old Filly.
- Royal Shake Em, a 1994 gray stallion by Royal Quick Dash, two-time stakes winner and the earner of $257,009.

And Easy Date, arguably Easy Jet's greatest daughter, did her part to add to the latter-day Merrick mix. Bred for the first time in 1977, the former All-American Futurity runner sent eight Merrick-bred performers to the tracks, including:

- Toast The Host, a 1983 sorrel stallion by Raise Your Glass (TB). SI 123, three-time stakes winner, earner of $57,725, 1986 Mexico Champion Racing Quarter Horse and 1986 Mexico Champion 3-Year-Old Colt.
- A Golden Date, a 1991 bay gelding by Bully Bullion. SI 103.
- Pastels, a 1990 sorrel mare by Six Fols. SI 100.
- Easy Date Dash, a 1992 sorrel mare by Dash For Cash. SI 97.
- Another Date, a 1978 bay mare by Hempen (TB). SI 95.
- Super De Easy, a 1994 sorrel stallion by Super De Kas. SI 95.
- Easy Caine, a 1982 sorrel stallion by Raise Caine (TB). SI 94.

Finally, there were Talking Picture and Sweet Illusion.

Talking Picture, a 1972 mare by Easy Jet and out of Lilly Lark by Lanolark, achieved a speed index of 91 and earned a Superior Race award. Retired to the Merrick broodmare band, she produced 10 runners with speed indexes of 90 or higher.

Sweet Illusion, a 1985 sorrel mare by Easy Jet and out of Mayflower Moon by Top Moon, achieved a speed index of 106, won two stakes races, and earned $62,724.

"Next to Top Date," Walter says, " Talking Picture and Sweet Illusion were two of my favorite Easy Jet mares.

"In my current broodmare band, I've got seven mares that I think are pretty nice. Two of them—Loquendi and A Royal Picture—are out of Talking Picture. Three more—Sweetly Special, Sweet Advice and Ms Optical Illusion—are out of Sweet Illusion.

"I've also got one last daughter of Easy Jet. Class Flirt is her name, and she's out of That's Classy (TB), by Our Hero by Bold Ruler. And I've got Falacy, a stakes-winning Thoroughbred daughter of Hempen.

"This year, Loquendi produced a sorrel colt by world champion runner Okey Dokey Dale, and Sweet Advice produced a sorrel colt by world champion runner Corona Cartel. Both colts are pretty nice, and I kinda go back and forth between them when it comes to which one I like best.

"They're part of the 62nd crop of Quarter Horse foals I've raised, and they sure look like prospects to me. I just hope I'm around long enough to see 'em run. I'm still as excited about getting 2-year-olds to the track as I was match racing Midnight Jr. as a 2-year-old in 1939.

"That part never changes, I guess. And who knows, maybe one of these colts will win the All-American for me."

*The Merrick-bred and owned Falacy (TB) was a stakes winner on the Thoroughbred tracks and the earner of a 92 speed index on the Quarter Horse tracks. She is shown here with jockey Vicky Smallwood in the irons.*

# 17

# THE LEGEND
# AND THE LEGACY

*At the prestigious $1.9 million 2001 All-American Futurity
in Ruidoso Downs—still the flagship event of the Quarter racing
industry—the first three finishers and seven of the 10 finalists
traced to Easy Jet and Midnight Jr.*

*A man and his horse…
hewn from the same
timber, born to the
same land, and forever
to be thought of as one.
In March 1993, at the
AQHA convention in
Albuquerque, New
Mexico, Walter
Merrick and Easy Jet
were both inducted
into the American
Quarter Horse
Association Hall of
Fame.*

*A man of few words, Walter managed to make a short speech of acceptance during the AQHA induction ceremony.*

**Photo by Dick Skrondahl - Far West**

FROM THE time he was 11 years old, Walter Merrick shouldered a man's load.

At first, his efforts helped provide staples for his aged parents. Later, they provided for his young family. Molded and hardened by this responsibility, early on in his life Walter developed into a self-starter, a hard-worker, a risk-taker and a visionary.

He also became a leader.

First, he simply led a couple of his young friends across the sparsely treed plains of south-central Colorado in search of mustang-hunting adventure and fun. Later, he led a small band of Davis Ranch cowboys in pursuit of a Depression-era livelihood. Finally, he helped lead the Quarter Horse racing industry from backwoods brush track infancy to front-page pari-mutuel maturity.

Walter probably never gave much thought to becoming a leader. It was simply an extension of the type of responsibility he had been raised to accept and make the best of. He was raised to be the man in charge.

It is small wonder then, that as Walter Merrick's life played out, he was consistently called upon to provide leadership and assume positions of authority. The list of roles that he filled includes:
- AQHA horse show judge.
- AQHA Director and member of the Show & Contest and Racing Committees.
- President and Director of the Oklahoma Quarter Horse Breeders Association.

*On November 16, 1981, Walter was inducted into the Oklahoma Hall of Fame—the only man to be so honored solely because of his accomplishments as a horseman. Here he is at the ceremony with Tien and Joe.*

**Photo by Paul E. Lefebvre**

- Co-owner and developer of the Haymaker Sales Company in Oklahoma City, Oklahoma.
- Charter member and co-owner of the Heritage Place sales pavilion in Oklahoma City.
- President of the Quarter Racing Owners of America (QROA) in 1972 and 1973.

As a result of a lifetime of dedication to and achievement within the Quarter Horse industry, Walter has received an even more impressive array of state and national honors. They include:

- 1979 Master Breeder award from Oklahoma State University at Stillwater.
- 1981 inductee into the Oklahoma Hall of Fame as one of 300 citizens who proved themselves as leaders in business, industry, military and government. He was the first man to be selected solely on his success in the Quarter Horse industry.
- 1981 AQHA Honorary Vice President.
- 1990 AQHA Legacy Award for 50 continuous years of breeding American Quarter Horses.
- 1993 inductee into the AQHA Hall of Fame. Easy Jet was inducted at the same time, and in 2002, Easy Date is slated to be inducted. The trio is the only breeder-sire-daughter team to be so honored.
- 2000 AQHA Racing Council Special Achievement Award.
- Honored as a "Living Legend" by the town of Sayre during its centennial celebration on September 15, 2001.

But the roles and awards pale in comparison to the legacy of Walter Merrick the horseman.

Beginning with Midnight Jr. in 1940 and continuing on with Gray Badger II, Three Bars, Bob's Folly, Lena's Bar, Little Lena Bars, Tonto Bars Hank, Jet Smooth, Easy Jet, Hempen and a host of other stallions and mares, the influence of Walter's intuitive efforts as a horse breeder have impacted virtually every corner of the Quarter Horse world.

To begin with, Walter's 1952

*At the 1972 Quarter Racing Owners of America (QROA) convention in El Paso, Texas, committee member Jack Scheiman presents Walter with a Meritorious Achievement Award.*

**Photo by Darst-Ireland Photography**

*At the same convention, Tien Merrick was presented a Randy Steffen bronze sculpture in recognition of her devotion to the racing industry and long-standing support of her husband.*

**Photo by Darst-Ireland Photography**

*Sunset Gallant Jet (foreground), a 1973 sorrel gelding by Easy Jet and out of Bold Jossette, achieved a speed index of 101 and earned a Superior Racehorse award. He then went on to become the 1979 and 1980 AQHA High Point Cutter & Chariot Horse.*

**Photo by Chapman's courtesy of Ron Carter**

discovery and subsequent promotion of Three Bars literally changed the course of Quarter Horse evolution.

On that subject alone, a separate book could be written. Suffice it to say that bringing Three Bars to Oklahoma and crossing him on the halter and working lines of Leo, Joe Hancock and Midnight Jr. resulted in a totally new and improved version of the American Quarter Horse—one that served as the prototype for the taller, stretchier, more-versatile Quarter Horse athlete of the 1960s and 1970s.

More than any other man and horse, Walter Merrick and Three Bars ushered in the benchmark era of the AQHA Supreme Champion—that ultimate equine competitor that performed well as a racehorse, cow horse, rail horse and halter horse.

Of the 44 Supreme Champions that were named between early 1967 and late 1972, 28 were Three Bars-bred. The first three to be named—Kid Meyers, Bar Money and Fairbars—were sons.

Had it not been for Walter Merrick's connection to Three Bars, it's doubtful that Bud Warren would have bred to him, and more doubtful that he would have sought out and purchased a Three Bars son—Sugar Bars—to breed to his Leo and Croton Oil mares. Had it not been for that cross, there would have been no Otoe, Classy Bars, or Bars Bailey lines to spearhead the spread of top all-around Quarter Horses into the Great Plains and the Northwest and Northeast sections of the country in the 1960s.

Had it not been for the Merrick-bred Three Bars son Steel Bars, there would have been no Joe Kirk Fulton-Aledo Bars line to streamline the look of the Quarter halter horse in the 1960s and 1970s.

And had it not been for Three Bars and Sugar Bars, there would be no Doc Bar, Jewel's Leo Bar, Zan Parr Bar or Shining Spark horses to raise the bar in the vast cutting, roping and reining horse industries of the 1970s,

1980s and 1990s. Nor would there have been an Impressive line to redefine the Quarter Horse halter industry in the 1980s and 1990s.

The Merrick-Three Bars influence extends even further.

Had it not been for Win Or Lose—a Three Bars grandson—being crossed on a Merrick-bred, line-bred Midnight Jr. mare named Chigger's Baby, there would have been no Sonny Dee Bar line of halter and pleasure horses. Furthermore, had it not been for the Walter Merrick-trained and campaigned Three Bars son Mighty Bars—a AAA, AQHA Champion—there would be no Quincy Dan or Sir Quincy Dan line of halter horses.

The Merrick-Midnight Jr. performance and racing line remains, if anything, even more influential.

Had it not been for the one-time Merrick-owned Midnight Jr. grandson Grey Badger III, there would be no

Two Eyed Jack or Peppy San Badger line of horses.

Had it not been for the Three Bars-Midnight Jr. granddaughter Miss Night Bar, there would be no Jet Deck, Jet Smooth or Easy Jet line of racehorses.

And the influence continues today.

In recent years, two Easy Jet sons—AQHA high-point cutter and chariot racer Sunset Gallant Jet, and PRCA bulldogging legend Cat Fish John—have served as classic examples that Merrick-bred speed will always be in style.

Every year, when the list of AQHA rodeo, race and performance high-point and Horse of the Year champions are named, the number that trace to Easy Jet or Midnight Jr. is consistently high.

At the prestigious $1.9 million 2001 All-American Futurity at Ruidoso Downs—still the indisputable

*Cat Fish John, a Merrick-bred 1972 chestnut gelding by Easy Jet and out of Lena's Bobby by Bob's Folly, achieved a speed index of 94. Sold by Walter to Alfalfa Feddersen of El Reno, Oklahoma, "Cat Fish" went to to become a multiple PRCA Steer Wrestling Horse of the Year.*

*Jim Merrick, Walter and Tien's oldest child, passed away of cancer on January 2, 1994, at the age of 60. He is shown here at a Montana branding in the early 1990s.*

flagship event of the Quarter racing industry—the first three finishers and seven of the 10 finalists traced to Easy Jet and Midnight Jr. Another two traced separately to Midnight Jr.

As far as the man behind the horses goes, life for Walter Merrick goes on today much as it has for the past eight decades.

As noted in the previous chapter, Walter still breeds Quarter Horse race prospects and still dreams of winning his third All-American.

Family ties remain of paramount importance. On October 6, 2001, Walter and Tien celebrated their 71st wedding anniversary. And, for the most part, the rest of the Merrick clan remains intact—and close.

*Here's the whole first- and second-generation Merrick clan, photographed on October 6, 1996, at Walt and Tien's 65th wedding anniversary party. In the front, from left, are Lynnie Merrick Suthers, Walter and Tien, and Joe Merrick. Standing in the back, from left, are Buddy Suthers, Donna Merrick Moss, Bob Moss and Sherry Merrick.*

One notable exception is Jim Merrick, Walter and Tien's oldest child. He passed away of cancer in 1994, at the age of 60. He is survived by two daughters—Lana Merrick and Gail Merrick Perry.

Donna Merrick Moss and husband Bob reside on the 14 Ranch. Between them, they have eight children—Rick, Kevin, Mark and Chip Anderson; Kimberly Anderson Staton; Misti Kohart; Micah Miller and Mandi Berry.

Lynnie Merrick Suthers and husband Buddy also reside on the ranch and have two sons, Destry and Ben.

Joe Merrick and wife Sherry live on the 14 Ranch and have one son, Kyle Walter, and two daughters, Kori and Kari.

Walter Merrick—the tall, unassuming young cowboy who just wanted to take care of his family and raise a few good horses—can look back from his current vantage-point at a life that has spanned 90 years.

And what a remarkable life it has been. Full of high drama, wide circles, peaks and valleys, and major accomplishments. The kind of life that few other men have lived.

Walter Merrick—cowboy, family man, match racer, horse breeder, living legend and national treasure.

Most surely, he is a child of the times and a man for all ages.

*On October 28, 2000, the AQHA Racing Council presented Walter with a Special Achievement Award "for a lifetime of outstanding service and dedication to the development, promotion and enhancement of American Quarter Horse Racing."*

# THROWIN' HORSESHOES
# AT THE MOON

*"Throwin' horseshoes at the moon, boys, it's mighty risky odds,*
*Sometimes you hook the Milky Way, or the outstretched hands of God.*
*But mostly they just fall to earth, in a dark and dusty hole,*
*And the sound of falling horseshoes, it pulls upon the soul."*

—*Tom Russell, from* The Man from God Knows Where
(c) 1999 High Tone Records

The cowboy headed slowly down the hill. More than usual this morning, his 90 years seemed to weigh heavily on his shoulders. Still tall and still possessing an imposing presence, he shuffled along with a noticeable limp—complements of a horseback spill and broken ankle suffered 75 years earlier.

"How did you sleep last night?" I asked.

"Not well," he said. "I don't sleep well anymore. I'm troubled by what I've done wrong."

The enormity of the statement caught me off guard. I was silent for a moment, then said the only thing that came to mind.

"Walter, what about what you've done right?"

Because any way you slice it, what you've done right far outweighs what you may have done wrong.

You've spent a lifetime on a land that has always demanded a certain hardiness of body and spirit of the soul of anyone who would call it home.

You've been married to the same woman for 71 years, you've raised a family that anyone would be proud of, and you've bred and raced some of the greatest horses that ever drew a breath. You dared shake your loop out large and toss it far, and you hooked more than your share of stars in the process.

It's been a good race, Walter—from wire to wire. One that few men could have run. And the track will always be better off for your having stepped on it.

# M E R R I C K   H O N O R   R O L L

### Merrick-bred AQHA Hall of Fame Horses

1. Easy Jet - 1993
2. Easy Date - 2002

### Merrick-bred World Champion Racehorses

1. Mona Leta - 1952 Co-Champion Three-Year-Old Filly
2. Easy Jet - 1969 Champion; Champion Stallion; Champion Two-Year-Old Colt
   1970 Champion Stallion; Champion Three-Year-Old Colt
3. Byou Bird - 1972 Champion Two-Year-Old Filly
4. Easy Date - 1974 Champion Two-Year-Old Filly
   1975 Champion; Champion Mare; Champion Three-Year-Old Filly
5. Liberty Coin - 1988 Champion Two-year-Old Gelding
7. Shake The Bank - 1995 Champion Two-Year-Old Filly

### Merrick-bred AQHA High-Point Racehorses

1. Easter Rose - 1956 High-Point Racehorse
2. Easy Jet - 1969 High Money Earning Horse
3. Easy Date - 1974 High Money Earning Horse

### Merrick-bred Superior Racehorses

1. Easter Rose
2. Tidy Bar
3. Jet Smooth
4. Mayflower Ann
5. Easy Jet
6. Byou Bird
7. Smoothly
8. Easy Date
9. Smooth Dun
10. Viva Villa
11. GentleOnMyMind
12. Jeb's Jet
13. Jet Equept
14. Surf King
15. Perfect Dial
16. Coda Mundi
17. First Session
18. Billingsley Punch
19. Native Host
20. Real Moody
21. Toast The Host
22. Liberty Coin
23. Shake The Bank
24. Royal Shake Em

### Merrick-bred AQHA High-Point Show Horses

1. Hank Will - 1972 High-Point Steer Roping Stallion

### Merrick-bred AQHA Supreme Champions

1. Bar Money
2. Hank Will

## Merrick-bred AQHA Champions

1. Leo Bingo
2. Miss Hi Jo
3. Bar Money
4. Jet Smooth
5. Hank Will
6. Scat Man Too
7. No Double

## Merrick-bred racehorse summary

568 starters - 7,810 starts
367 winners - 1,275 wins
40 stakes winners - 105 stakes wins
385 total ROMs
162 ROMs of 90+
54 ROMs of 100+
26 Superior Race Awards
6 World Champions - 13 World
    Championships
Money Earned: $6,393,321

## Merrick-bred Superior Show Horses

1. Leo Bingo (halter)
2. Duck Call (halter)
3. Lucky 14 (halter)
4. Lucky 14 (western pleasure)
5. Mr Scat Man (halter)
6. Present Me (western pleasure)
7. Final Point (barrel racing)

## Merrick-bred show horse summary

28 halter point earners - 816 points
    four Superior Halter Awards
46 performance point earners -
    662.5 points,
    25 ROMs
    3 Superior Performance Awards.

*Easy Jet, Walter Merrick and Jet Smooth — their impact on the Western Horse has been profound.*

**Photo by Walt Wiggins, Sr.**

# EASY JET HONOR ROLL

## SIRE

### World Champions

1. Easy Date - 1974 Champion Two-Year-Old Filly; 1975 Champion; Champion Mare; Champion Three-Year-Old Filly
2. Megahertz - 1976 Champion Two-Year-Old Colt
3. My Easy Credit - 1977 Champion Three-Year-Old; Champion Three-Year-Old Colt
4. Easy Move - 1978 Champion Three-Year-Old Colt
5. Easy Angel - 1979 Champion Two-Year-Old; Champion Two-Year-Old Filly
6. Sunset Gallant Jet - 1979 High Point Cutter & Chariot; 1980 High Point Cutter and Chariot
7. Extra Easy - 1980 Champion Three-Year-Old Colt *- Jet Dance ran again? him L,A!*
8. Pie In The Sky - 1979 Champion Two-Year-Old Colt
9  Easily Smashed - 1981 Champion Three-Year-Old Colt
10. Shoot Yeah - 1987 Champion Two-Year-Old Colt

### All-American Futurity Winners

1. Easy Date - 1974
2. PieInTheSky-1979
3. MrTruckaJet- 1985

### Top 10 Money Earners

1. Mr Trucka Jet - $1,033,115
2. Easy Date - $849,710
3. Teller Queen - $637,917
4. Pie In The Sky - $616,328
5. My Easy Credit - $502,504
6. Easy Angel - $477,634
7. Easy Treasure - $361,748
8. Easily Smashed - $326,060
9. Freedom Flyer - $309,008
10. Shoot Yeah - $304,143

```
                               ┌ Top Deck (TB)
                  ┌ Moon Deck ─┤
                  │            └ Moonlight Night
     ┌ Jet Deck ──┤
     │            │                ┌ Barred
     │            └ Miss Night Bar ┤
Easy Jet ─┤                        └ Belle of Midnight
     │
     │                        ┌ Percentage (TB)
     │            ┌ Three Bars (TB) ┤
     │            │           └ Myrtle Dee (TB)
     └ Lena's Bar (TB) ┤
                  │           ┌ Gray Dream (TB)
                  └ Lena Valenti (TB) ┤
                              └ Perhobo (TB)
```

## Maternal Grandsire

### World Champions

1. Eastex - 1984 Champion Two-Year-Old; Champion Two-Year-Old Gelding
2. Rise N High - 1984 Champion Three-Year-Old Gelding
3. Easygo Effort - 1987 Champion Two-Year-Old Gelding
4. Takin On The Cash - 1990 Champion Two-Year-Old Colt;
     1991 Champion Three-Year-Old; Champion Three-Year-Old Colt
5. Casadys Capter - 1990 High Point Cutter & Chariot; High Point Sr Cutter &
     Chariot 1991 High Point Cutter & Chariot; High Point Sr Cutter & Chariot
7. Im Johnnys Jet - 1990 High Point Jr Cutter & Chariot
6. Four Forty Blast - 1993 Champion Three-Year-Old Gelding
7. Fabulous Form - 1997 Champion Three-Year-Old Filly
8. Dashing Perfection - 1997 Champion Three-Year-Old;
     Champion Three-Year-Old Gelding
9. Go Larkingly - 1997 World Champion Chariot Racing Team

### All-American Futurity Winners

1. Eastex - 1984

### Top 10 Money Earners

1. Eastex - $1,869,406
2. Mine Cash - $1,142,428
3. Takin On The Cash - $661,697
4. Meganette - $657,620
5. Dashing Perfection - $553,644
6. Rise N High - $522,075
7. Such An Easy Effort - $496,127
8. Easygo Effort - $431,551
9. Digging For Gold - $426,086
10. Rolls Of Romance - $365,222

*Easy Jet and Willy Lovell — together they made Quarter Racing history.*

# Photo Index

# AUTHOR'S PROFILE

FRANK HOLMES has been penning horse-related feature articles and historical books for more than 35 years. His interests have always been centered on the historical aspects of the western horse breeds, and his broad-based knowledge of the origins of the Quarter Horse, Paint, Appaloosa, and Palomino registries have established him as one of the pre-eminent equine historians of all time.

As a former staff writer for *Western Horseman* magazine, Frank co-authored volumes 2 through 5 of the popular Legends book series and authored *The Hank Wiescamp Story*.

As the award-winning Features Editor of *The Paint Horse Journal*, he contributed a consistent stream of top-notch personality profiles, genetic studies, and historical overviews.

From early 2001 on, Frank has devoted most of his journalistic efforts to the research and writing of historical books designed to capture the West's rich history and pass it on in a way that both enlightens and entertains.

Now living near Colorado Springs, Colorado, he has two sons, Eric and Craig.